GCSE german for OCR

Grammar Workbook

Michael Spencer

OCR
RECOGNISING ACHIEVEMENT

OXFORD
UNIVERSITY PRESS

Official Publisher Partnership

UNIVERSITY PRESS

Great Clarendon Street, Oxford OX2 6DP

Oxford University Press is a department of the University of Oxford.

It furthers the University's objective of excellence in research,
scholarship, and education by publishing worldwide in

Oxford   New York
Auckland   Cape Town   Dar es Salaam   Hong Kong   Karachi
Kuala Lumpur   Madrid   Melbourne   Mexico City   Nairobi
New Delhi   Shanghai   Taipei   Toronto

With offices in

Argentina   Austria   Brazil   Chile   Czech Republic   France   Greece
Guatemala   Hungary   Italy   Japan   South Korea   Poland   Portugal
Singapore   Switzerland   Thailand   Turkey   Ukraine   Vietnam

Oxford is a registered trade mark of Oxford University Press
in the UK and in certain other countries

British Library Cataloguing in Publication Data

Data available

ISBN 978 019 915492 0

10 9 8 7 6

Printed in Great Britain by Ashford Colour Press Ltd

Paper used in the production of this book is a natural,
recyclable product made from wood grown in sustainable forests.
The manufacturing process conforms to the environmental regulations
of the country of origin.

Acknowledgements
Cover image: Erik Isakson/Getty

The authors and publishers would like to thank Katie Lewis and
Marion Dill for their help and advice.

Every effort has been made to contact copyright holders of material
reproduced in this book. If notified, the publishers
will be pleased to rectify any errors or omissions at the
earliest opportunity.

Contents

Cases

1 Underline the nouns in one colour and the pronouns in another colour in the following sentences.

  a Ich habe ein tolles Zimmer, wo ich meine Hausaufgaben mache.

  b Mein Bruder hat ein ziemlich kleines Zimmer mit einem Einbauschrank.

  c Er hört dort Musik und ich spiele mit ihm am Computer.

  d Wir haben eine große Küche, wo ich immer frühstücke.

  e Wir haben auch einen schönen Garten mit vielen Blumen.

  f Wir haben zwei Hunde. Jeden Tag gehe ich mit ihnen spazieren.

  g Nach dem Abendessen sehe ich meistens ein bisschen fern.

Nominative

TIPP

Use the **nominative case** for the subject of a verb. The subject is the person or thing 'doing' the action of the verb.

2 Underline the words that are the subject of these sentences.

  a Mein Bruder hat viele Filme.

  b Ich sehe deine Schwester im Park.

  c Machst du deine Hausaufgaben?

  d Unsere Großeltern haben ein schönes Haus.

  e Thomas hat sein neues Buch schon gelesen.

  f Wo ist dein Zimmer?

  g Normalerweise kommen Mutti und Vati um 18 Uhr nach Hause.

  h Nach der Schule sehen mein Bruder und ich fern.

TIPP

Always use the nominative case after the verbs *sein*, *werden* and *bleiben*.

3 Choose the correct word from the pair given in brackets.

  a Das ist (mein/meinen) älterer Bruder.

  b Er wird ein (berühmten/berühmter) Fußballspieler.

  c Anja und Lena sind (unsere/unseren) besten Freundinnen.

  d Max ist nett, aber Thomas bleibt (mein/meinen) bester Freund.

  e Meine Schwester ist (keine/kein) schlechte Tennisspielerin geworden, finde ich.

  f Sie war früher (eine/einer) bekannte Sportlerin.

4 Write down four different subject pronouns and four noun phrases in the nominative case as prompted in brackets. Then write a sentence for each of the words and phrases.

pronouns	noun phrases
e.g. *ich*	*mein bester Freund*

  a _____   e _____

  b _____   f _____

  c _____   g _____

  d _____   h _____

  a _____

  b _____

  c _____

  d _____

  e _____

  f _____

  g _____

  h _____

Accusative

The **accusative case** is used for the direct object of a verb. The direct object is the person or thing having the action of the verb 'done' to it.

Remember that some verbs do not have a direct object, e.g. verbs of motion.

1 Underline the words that are the direct object of these sentences.

   a Meine Schwestern haben viele Computerspiele.

   b Ich sehe deinen Bruder in der Sporthalle.

   c Warum macht ihr eure Hausaufgaben nicht?

   d Unsere Freunde werden ein schönes Haus kaufen.

   e Ich habe das große Buch schon gelesen.

   f Hat Max diese CD schon gehört?

   g Im Sommer spiele ich sehr gern Tennis.

   h Zum Geburtstag hat mir meine Tante eine Jacke gegeben.

   i Heike fährt in die Stadt und kauft sich einen Pullover.

   j Sie ist ins Kaufhaus gegangen, hat aber nichts Passendes gefunden.

Many time phrases are in the accusative case.

2 Translate these phrases into German.

   a last week   letzt_____ W_____

   b next Tuesday   nä_____ D_____

   c next month   n_____ M_____

   d last Friday   le_____ F_____

   e last year   _____ J_____

Always use the accusative case after these prepositions:

durch	through
für	for
gegen	against (position, versus)
ohne	without
um	around, about
wider	against (contrary to)
entlang	along

(See page 14 for further practice.)

3 Translate into English.

   a für meinen Vater   _____

   b durch die Stadt   _____

   c ohne sein Fahrrad   _____

   d die Hauptstraße entlang _____

   e gegen die Wand   _____

   f um den Parkplatz   _____

You use the accusative case after these prepositions if there is a change of place or state involved:

an	at, on(to)
auf	on(to)
hinter	behind
in	in(to)
neben	next to, near
über	over
unter	under
vor	before, in front of
zwischen	between

(See page 16 for further practice.)

4 Underline the phrases that are in the accusative case.

   a Bitte stell die Bücher auf den Tisch!

   b Das Schwimmbad ist neben dem Stadion am Stadtrand.

   c Wir gehen gleich in die Sporthalle.

   d Es ist schwierig, wenn man immer im Restaurant essen muss.

   e Vor dem Rathaus gehst du über eine Brücke.

   f Die meisten Menschen werden beim Himalaya an die hohen Berge denken.

Genitive

1 Translate into English.

a der Titel des Buches _____

b die Stimme des Lehrers _____

c das Auto meiner Mutter _____

d der Tennisspieler des Jahres _____

e der Anfang der Prüfungen _____

2 Look at the examples in Exercise 1 and complete the
explanation.

Masculine and neuter nouns which have one

_____ add –*es* in the genitive singular.

Add just –*s* in the genitive _____ for masculine

and neuter nouns with _____ or more

_____ .

_____ and plural nouns do not change in the

genitive case.

| Feminine singular syllable syllables two |

3 Rewrite these phrases in English, then translate them
into German.

e.g. my friend's car = *the car of my friend* = *das Auto
meines Freundes*

a my sister's bike = _____

= _____

b his grandparents' house = _____

= _____

c this school's motto = _____

= das Motto _____

d he has his brother's computer

= _____

= er hat den _____

e in my friend's car = _____

= mit _____

4 Choose one of the above prepositions to fill each gap.

a Wir wohnen etwas _____ der Stadt.

b Das Spiel war _____ des schlechten Wetters
total ruiniert.

c Was machst du _____ der Pause?

d _____ des schlechten Wetters haben wir viel
Spaß gehabt.

e Er nimmt seine Freundin _____ seiner kleinen
Schwester mit.

Dative

1 Match the German to the English. Then underline the indirect object in each sentence.

1 Der Koch gab der Katze einen Fisch.	**a** I'm telling the children a story.
2 Frau Fischer kauft mir eine Katze.	**b** Are you sending your friend an email?
3 Ich erzähle den Kindern eine Geschichte.	**c** He wrote the headmaster a letter.
4 Er schrieb dem Direktor einen Brief.	**d** The cook gave the cat a fish.
5 Schickst du deinem Freund eine E-Mail?	**e** Give the lady your email address.
6 Gib der Dame deine E-Mail-Adresse!	**f** Mrs Fisher is buying me a cat.

2 Translate into English.

a mit meinen Freunden _____

b gegenüber der Bank _____

c nach einer Stunde _____

d aus dem Garten _____

e bei unserer Oma _____

f die Mutter von meiner Freundin _____

3 Underline the phrases that are in the dative case.

a Das Restaurant war hinter dem Rathaus.

b Als Skilehrer bin ich stundenlang auf den Pisten.

c Lies diese Broschüre über gesundes Essen!

d Wir stehen vor dem Kino und warten.

e Ich freue mich auf die Sommerferien.

f Sein Foto hängt an der Wand.

4 Underline the dative case in each sentence, then, on separate paper, translate into English.

a Der blaue Rock passt meiner Schwester nicht.

b Ich glaube dir nicht!

c Wir dankten dem Gruppenleiter.

d Kannst du mir bitte helfen?

e Er folgte den Spielern ins Stadion.

f Diese Geschichte gefällt mir nicht.

Nouns

What is a noun?

1 Circle the nouns and translate them into English.

a Beruf _____

b böse _____

c danken _____

d Empfangsdame _____

e funktionieren _____

f Größe _____

g Hauptstraße _____

h Informatik _____

i leicht _____

j Schlafsack _____

k weniger _____

l Zwiebel _____

Gender

Masculine (*der*)	Feminine (*die*)	Neuter (*das*)
–er	–e	–chen
–ig	–in, –ion	–lein
–ist	–ik	–um, –ium
–ant	–heit, –keit	many ending –el, –en
–us, –ismus	–schaft	many adopted from other languages
some ending –el, –en	–ung	many beginning Ge-

2 Write *der*, *die* or *das* in front of the following nouns without looking them up. Then check in a dictionary to see whether you are correct.

a _____ Fabrik

b _____ Gemüse

c _____ Prüfung

d _____ Mädchen

e _____ Schule

f _____ Bäcker

g _____ Seekrankheit

h _____ Nation

i _____ Zentrum

j _____ Verkäuferin

k _____ Einladung

l _____ Freundschaft

3 In each group of words, underline the one that has a different gender from the others. Check that you know the meaning of all the words.

a Mutter, Vater, Tochter, Schwester

b Gepäck, Gemüse, Gebäude, Geburtstag

c Kindheit, Krankenhaus, Krankheit, Gesundheit

d Ingenieurin, Polizist, Gemüsehändler, Tennisspieler

e Hähnchen, Würstchen, Hase, Kaninchen

f Ordnung, Restaurant, Operation, Musik

g Gebiet, Gehalt, Geige, Geschäft

h Skigebiet, Skischule, Skilehrerin, Skihose

Singular and plural

1 Try to add an example to each category listed.

a Most feminine nouns add *-n, -en* or *-nen*:

die Pflanze, die Pflanze**n** _____

die Prüfung, die Prüfung**en** _____

die Lehrerin, die Lehrerin**nen** _____

b Most masculine nouns add *-e*. Many put an Umlaut on the main vowel as well:

der Arm, die Arm**e** _____

der Stuhl, die Stüh**le** _____

c Most neuter nouns add *-er* and put an Umlaut on the main vowel:

das Schloss, die Schlöss**er** _____

d Many foreign words add *-s*:

das Büro, die Büro**s** _____

e Most masculine and neuter nouns ending in *-el, -en, -er, -chen* and *-lein* stay the same:

der Onkel, die Onkel _____

das Mittel, die Mittel _____

der Wagen, die Wagen _____

das Treffen, die Treffen _____

der Lehrer, die Lehrer _____

das Zimmer, die Zimmer _____

das Kaninchen, die Kaninchen _____

f Some masculine nouns ending in *-el, -en, -er* just add an Umlaut:

der Vater, die V**ä**ter _____

g Neuter nouns ending in *-um* change this to *-en*:

das Zentrum, die Zentr**en** _____

2 Write these nouns in the plural. Check in a dictionary.

a das Meerschweinchen _____

b die Karte _____

c das Fach _____

d der Schläger _____

e das Baby _____

f der Geburtstag _____

g der Hügel _____

h die Köchin _____

i das Gasthaus _____

j der Fuß _____

k die Zeitung _____

3 Write these nouns in the singular and give the gender. Check in a dictionary.

a Bahnhöfe der _____

b Digitalkameras die _____

c Stiefel _____

d Übernachtungen _____

e Turnschuhe _____

f Verkäuferinnen _____

g Würstchen _____

h Katzen _____

i Daten _____

j Autofahrer _____

k Jugendzentren _____

4 Write these phrases in the plural.

a mit dem Hund mit den _____

b aus dem Haus _____

c in der Schule _____

d von diesem Mädchen _____

e hinter dem Hotel _____

Nouns from adjectives

e fremd (*a foreign girl*) _____

f klug (*the clever lady*) _____

TIPP

In German, nouns can be made from **adjectives**: *deutsch – ein Deutscher* (German – a German), *gut – das Gute* (good – the good), *jugendlich – die Jugendlichen* (youthful – young people).

1 Underline the adjectival noun in each sentence and state what case each one is in (**N, A, G** or **D**).

a Hast du den Alten gesehen? _____

b Die Armen haben heute eine Prüfung. _____

c Wir fahren mit Verwandten nach Berlin. _____

d Er möchte eine Reiche kennenlernen. _____

e Ich kenne viele Deutsche. _____

f Er hat dem Beamten seinen Pass gezeigt. _____

TIPP

These nouns are often made from the superlative form of the adjective: *das Beste* (the best), *das Schlechteste* (the worst), *das Längste* (the longest).

2 Write the adjective from which each noun has been formed and also its meaning:

e.g. *das Längste – lang – long*

a das Wichtigste _____

b das Interessanteste _____

c der Größte _____

d die Kleinsten _____

e die Toten _____

3 Form nouns from these adjectives. (See pages 21–23 for help with the adjective endings.)

a bekannt (*a male acquaintance*) ein _____

b deutsch (*the Germans*) _____

c krank (*a sick man*) _____

d weiß (*the white one (rabbit)*) _____

Weak nouns

TIPP

Some masculine nouns are known as **'weak' nouns**. They add *-n* or *-en* in all except the nominative singular. Weak nouns are usually people and occasionally animals. They often designate men in particular positions or professions: e.g. *Herr, Junge, Mensch, Neffe, Affe, Löwe, Kollege, Kamerad, Student, Polizist, Tourist, Name.*

They follow the pattern shown in the following table.

	Singular	**Plural**
Nominative	der Junge/Student	die Jungen/ Studenten
Accusative	den Jungen/ Studenten	die Jungen/ Studenten
Genitive	des Jungen/ Studenten	der Jungen/ Studenten
Dative	dem Jungen/ Studenten	den Jungen/ Studenten

4 Complete the sentences with the correct endings for the weak nouns (if they need an ending).

a Der Student_____ hat seinem Kamerad_____ eine Postkarte geschickt.

b Er gibt Herr_____ Büddig sein Heft.

c Sein Neffe_____ ist der Sohn eines Kollege_____.

d Unter den Tourist_____ haben wir einen berühmten Mensch_____ gesehen.

e Im Zoo haben wir einen Bär_____, viele Affe_____ und einen Löwe_____ gefüttert.

f Der Junge_____ hat den Name_____ eines anderen Student_____ geschrieben.

Determiners

What is a determiner?

A **determiner** is a word like 'the', 'a', 'my', 'this' when used in front of a noun. It changes according to the gender, number and case of the noun.

Definite article ['the']

The words for 'the' (**definite article**) follow the pattern in the table.

1 Use the sentences beneath the table to help complete it.

	Masculine	Feminine	Neuter	Plural
Nominative	der		das	
Accusative		die		die
Genitive	des	der		der
Dative			dem	

a Die Schule endet um 13 Uhr.
b Die Farbe des Autos gefällt mir.
c Nimm das Glas und trink den Saft.
d Die Kinder essen gern Gemüse.
e Ich wohne in der Stadtmitte und fahre immer mit dem Bus.
f In den Supermärkten kann man fast alles kaufen.

Sometimes, a definite or indefinite article is used in English when one is not needed in German:
- with professions and nationalities (unless there is an adjective): *Sie ist Ärztin* (aber *Sie ist eine gute Ärztin*)
- with musical instruments: *Spielst du Klavier?*
- with some expressions for illness: *Ich habe Fieber/ Magenschmerzen.*

Indefinite article ['a'] and 'no'

The words for 'a' (**indefinite article**) follow the pattern given in the table. There is no plural of 'a' but *kein* ('not a', 'no') follows the same pattern and it does have a plural.

	Masculine	Feminine	Neuter	Plural
Nominative	ein/kein	eine/ keine	ein/kein	keine
Accusative	einen/ keinen	eine/ keine	ein/kein	keine
Genitive	eines/ keines	einer/ keiner	eines/ keines	keiner
Dative	einem/ keinem	einer/ keiner	einem/ keinem	keinen

2 Complete the sentences with the correct form of *ein* and *kein*. To help you, the gender (m, f, n) and case (N, A, G, D) are given in brackets.

a Es gibt e_____ Konzert in der Mitte e_____ Parks. (n A, m G)

b Man spielt „E_____ kleine Nachtmusik" von Mozart. (f A)

c Ich gehe mit e_____ Gruppe aus e_____ Musikverein dorthin. (f D, m D)

d Ich spiele k_____ Instrument, aber Musik gefällt mir. (n A)

e Ich höre k_____ Rock und k_____ Technobands. (m A, pl A)

3 Translate into German.

a She is *a* German. _____

b Herr Schmidt is *a* baker. _____

c I play *the* clarinet. _____

d Have you got *a* temperature? _____

e She has *a* headache. _____

Possessive adjectives ('my', 'your' etc.)

Possessive adjectives are *mein* (my), *dein* (your), *sein* (his, its), *ihr* (her, its, their), *unser* (our), *euer* (your) and *Ihr* (your). They follow the same pattern as *ein* and *kein*.

Note that when using *euer*, the second –e– is usually missed out in all except the masculine nominative and the neuter nominative and accusative.

To sum up how to say 'your':

* Use *dein* for people you address as *du* (familiar form singular).
* Use *euer* for the familiar plural (people you address as *ihr*).
* Use *Ihr* for the polite form (people you address as *Sie*).

See page 37 for further practice.

1 Complete the tables.

	Masculine	Feminine	Neuter	Plural
Nominative	mein			meine
Accusative				
Genitive				
Dative				

	Masculine	Feminine	Neuter	Plural
Nominative	ihr			ihre
Accusative				
Genitive				
Dative				

	Masculine	Feminine	Neuter	Plural
Nominative	unser			unsere
Accusative				
Genitive				
Dative				

	Masculine	Feminine	Neuter	Plural
Nominative	euer	eure		eure
Accusative	euren			eure
Genitive				
Dative				

2 Translate into German (nominative case).

a my house   _____

b his mother   _____

c your (*du* form) friends _____

d her parents   _____

e our school   _____

f their money   _____

g your (*Sie* form) job   _____

h its (= the cat's) toy   _____

i its (= the dog's) rug   _____

j your (*ihr* form) books _____

3 Choose three of the phrases in Exercise 2 and put each of them into a sentence using a different case each time:

e.g. (dative) (**a**) *Ich habe sechs Zimmer in meinem Haus.*

(accusative) _____

_____

_____

(genitive) _____

_____

_____

(dative) _____

_____

_____

dieser, jener, jeder ('this', 'that', 'every')

1 Complete the tables. The sentences that follow them will help you. Then translate each sentence into English.

	Masculine	Feminine	Neuter	Plural
Nominative	dieser		dieses	
Accusative		diese		diese
Genitive	dieses	dieser	dieses	dieser
Dative	diesem			

	Masculine	Feminine	Neuter	Plural
Nominative		jene		
Accusative	jenen			
Genitive		jener	jenes	
Dative			jenem	jenen

	Masculine	Feminine	Neuter
Nominative		jede	jedes
Accusative			
Genitive		jeder	jedes
Dative	jedem		

a Jede Woche lernen wir etwas Neues aus diesem Buch.

_____

b Es ist in jedem guten Geschäft zu kaufen.

_____

c Hast du dieses Magazin schon gelesen?

_____

d Jeder Schüler in jeder Schule soll diesen Film sehen.

_____

e Diese Vorstellung ist nicht für jedes Kind geeignet.

_____

f Die Eltern jedes Schülers in dieser Gruppe entscheiden.

_____

g Diese armen Leute arbeiten jeden Tag in diesen Ländern.

_____

h Ich bin in jener Kleinstadt aufgewachsen.

_____

Interrogative adjective ('which')

	Masculine	Feminine	Neuter	Plural
Nominative	welcher	welche	welches	welche
Accusative	welchen	welche	welches	welche
Genitive	welches	welcher	welches	welcher
Dative	welchem	welcher	welchem	welchen

2 Complete the questions with the correct form of *welcher* each time. The case (N, A, G, D) is given to help you.

a W_____ Produkte sind billig? (N)

b W_____ Sportart ziehst du vor? (A)

c W_____ Film habt ihr gestern gesehen? (A)

d Mit w_____ Bus fahren wir in die Stadt? (D)

e In w_____ Geschäften kaufst du am liebsten ein? (D)

f W_____ Kind hat die beste Stimme? (N)

g Aus w_____ Grund sagst du das? (D)

h Durch w_____ Eingang sind Sie gekommen? (A)

Prepositions

What is a preposition?

1 Underline the prepositions (in English and German), draw lines to join the pairs, then write which case (A, G, D) is used with each German preposition.

e.g. I'm going <u>by</u> car.

1 We drove through the town.
2 It's on the table.
3 because of the rain
4 without my mother
5 He's sitting between the trees.
6 instead of my brother
7 a book by my uncle
8 before the game
9 Come after lunch.
10 Jump into the lake!
11 in my opinion

a statt meines Bruders ____
b wegen des Regens ____
c Ich fahre <u>mit</u> dem Auto. _D_
d meiner Meinung nach ____
e Komm nach dem Mittagessen! ____
f Es ist auf dem Tisch. ____
g Spring in den See! ____
h Er sitzt zwischen den Bäumen. ____
i Wir fuhren durch die Stadt. ____
j ohne meine Mutter ____
k vor dem Spiel ____
l ein Buch von meinem Onkel ____

Prepositions with the accusative case

2 Translate these phrases into German.

a for his sister _____

b against a tree _____

c along the motorway _____

d around the town _____

e through the door _____

f without her friends _____

g against the boys _____

h round the table _____

3 Make up sentences in German using each of the phrases in Exercise 2.

a _____

b _____

c _____

d _____

e _____

f _____

g _____

h _____

Prepositions with the dative case

These prepositions are **always** followed by the **dative case**:

aus	out of
außer	except for
bei	at the house of
mit	with, by
nach	to, after
seit	since, for (time)
von	from, of, by
zu	to, at
gegenüber	opposite

Er kommt aus einer Kleinstadt und fährt immer mit dem Bus. Er sitzt mir gegenüber.
He comes from a small town and always travels by bus. He is sitting opposite me.

Note that *gegenüber* sometimes goes after the noun or pronoun.

1 Put one of the above prepositions into each gap.

a Ich bleibe eine Woche _____ meinen Großeltern.

b Er ist krank und darf nicht _____ dem Haus gehen.

c _____ wie vielen Jahren lernst du Deutsch?

d Mein Vater wurde drei Jahre _____ meiner Mutter geboren.

e Wann gehst du _____ deiner Tante?

f Unser Klassenzimmer liegt _____ den Toiletten.

g Kommst du _____ meinen Freunden zum Freibad?

h Wir fahren morgen _____ Berlin.

i _____ mir hat jedes Kind genug Geld.

j Das Buch ist _____ einem berühmten Deutschen.

Note that *bei dem* and *von dem* can be shortened to *beim* and *vom* and *zu dem* and *zu der* can be shortened to *zum* and *zur*.

2 Complete the sentences with the shortened versions.

a Er ist heute _____ Arzt.

b Samstags gehen wir immer _____ Supermarkt.

c Sonntags gehen wir nicht _____ Schule.

d Dieses Jahr fahren wir _____ 20. Juli _____ 11. August weg.

e Ich habe das Spiel _____ Bruder meines Freundes gekauft.

f _____ Bäcker im Dorf gibt es tolles Brot.

There is a special use of *seit* with the present and imperfect tenses:

*Ich **wohne seit** 10 Jahren hier.*
I **have lived** here **for** 10 years.

Note that we use the present tense in German, but the past tense in English. Ask yourself whether the action is still going on. Are you still living in the same place now (in the present)? Yes – so use the **present** tense.

*Er **spielte** schon **seit** zwei Stunden, als es begann zu schneien.*
He **had** already **been playing for** two hours when it began to snow.

Here, we are using the imperfect tense in German, but the pluperfect in English, i.e. He *was* **still playing** when the snow started, so use the **imperfect** tense.

3 On separate paper, translate into English.

a Da bist du ja endlich! Ich warte seit 10 Minuten hier in der Kälte.

b Ich wartete seit einer Stunde in der Kälte und meine Schwester kam immer noch nicht.

c Wir lernen seit drei Jahren Deutsch.

d Wir lernten seit drei Jahren Deutsch und konnten schon ziemlich viel verstehen.

e Sie ist seit vier Jahren Sängerin in einer Band.

f Sie war seit vier Jahren Sängerin, hatte aber nie in einer Band gesungen.

Prepositions with either accusative or dative case

These prepositions can be followed by the **accusative case** or the **dative case**, depending on the meaning:

an	at, on(to)
auf	on(to)
hinter	behind
in	in(to)
neben	next to, near
über	over
unter	under
vor	before, in front of
zwischen	between

They take the accusative if there is a change of place (movement) or state.

Sie legt das Buch auf den Tisch.
She's putting the book on the table. (change of place)

They take the dative if they describe position and there is **no** change of place or state.

Das Buch ist auf dem Tisch.
The book is on the table. (no change of place)

1 In each pair of sentences, there is one example of the accusative used with movement and one example of the dative used with position. Write A (accusative) or D (dative) next to each sentence.

a Häng das Poster bitte an die Wand! _____

Dieses Poster hängt schon seit zwei Jahren an der Wand. _____

b Meine Schulbücher liegen auf dem Schreibtisch. _____

Ich habe meine Schulbücher auf den Schreibtisch gelegt. _____

c Wir sollen hinter dem Supermarkt parken. _____

Wir sollen hinter den Supermarkt fahren. _____

d Sie fliegt gern ins Ausland. _____

Sie wohnt gern im Ausland. _____

e Stell das Eis nicht neben den Ofen! _____

Oh je! Das Eis ist neben dem Ofen. _____

f Siehst du den Hubschrauber im Himmel über dem Krankenhaus? _____

Der Hubschrauber ist zweimal über unser Haus geflogen. _____

g Eine Maus ist unter den Schrank gelaufen. _____

Er hat eine tote Maus unter dem Schrank gefunden. _____

h Er fährt das Auto aus der Garage und vor das Haus. _____

Unser Auto steht vor dem Haus. _____

i Der Lehrer steht zwischen den Tischen. _____

Er stellt einen Stuhl zwischen die Tische. _____

Note that *in dem* and *an dem* (dative) can be shortened to *im* and *am* and *in das* and *an das* (accusative) can be shortened to *ins* and *ans*.

2 Fill the gaps with the correct shortened version. The case is given to help you.

a Ich wohne _____ Stadtrand. (D)

b Wir sind _____ Wasser gesprungen. (A)

c Im Sommer will ich _____ Meer fahren. (A)

d Kommst du mit _____ Kino? (A)

e Mein Bruder arbeitet _____ Supermarkt. (D)

f _____ Wochenende laufen wir Ski. (D)

3 The Müller family have a new cleaning lady. Circle the correct alternative in each of these instructions to her.

a Der Staubsauger ist (in den/im) Keller.

b Bitte stecken Sie das rote T-Shirt nicht in (die/der) Waschmaschine!

c Das Waschmittel ist (in den/im) Schrank neben (die/der) Waschmaschine.

d Hängen Sie bitte die Wäsche auf (die/der) Leine (in den/im) Garten.

e Stellen Sie bitte den Mülleimer vor (das/dem) Haus.

f Vorsicht! Markus hat viel schmutzige Wäsche unter (sein/seinem) Bett.

g Bitte tun Sie das Spielzeug in (die/den) Schränke im Kinderzimmer.

h Der Hund soll (in den/im) Garten bleiben. Wenn es regnet, darf er (ins/im) Haus kommen.

4 Translate the pairs of sentences into English. Pay careful attention to the cases used.

a Wir sind in die Stadtmitte gefahren.

_____

Wir sind in der Stadtmitte herumgefahren.

_____

b Er setzte sich ans Fenster.

_____

Er sitzt am Fenster.

_____

c Ein Flugzeug fliegt alle 10 Minuten über die Schule.

_____

Die Flugzeuge sind so laut, wenn sie direkt über der Schule sind.

_____

d Unsere Katze schläft unter meinem Bett.

_____

Jeden Abend um 10 Uhr kriecht* die Katze unter mein Bett.

_____

[*kriechen = to creep]

5 Fill in the gaps.

a Bring die Limoflaschen bitte in _____ Keller.

b Es gibt keinen Parkplatz hinter _____ Supermarkt. Du musst i_____ Parkhaus parken.

c Jeden Abend arbeite ich an mein_____ Computer.

d Normalerweise fahre ich vor _____ Rathaus und dann über _____ Brücke.

e Das Museum liegt zwischen _____ Kirche und ein_____ Sportgeschäft.

f Ich gehe in _____ Sporthalle, die neben _____ Tennisplätzen ist.

6 Now complete the summary using the words in the box.

Some (1) _____ use either the accusative case or the dative case depending on their meaning.

If there is (2) _____ involved (e.g. something changes place), use the (3) _____ case – (4) _____, *die, das* etc. For example, if you put a pen onto a table, (5) _____ a bag, under your chair etc., it has moved from your hand to that other place so you must use the accusative case: *Ich lege den Kuli auf den Tisch*.

If you are describing the (6) _____ of something and there is no change of (7) _____, use the (8) _____ case – *dem, der*, (9) _____ etc. For example, if you are saying that a pen is on the table, in your bag, under a chair etc., it isn't moving from one place to (10) _____, so you use the dative case: *Der Kuli liegt auf dem Tisch*.

Remember that this only applies to the group of prepositions where you have a (11) _____ of accusative or dative. The ones that always take the accusative or (12) _____ take the dative are not affected.

| accusative always another choice |
| dative *dem den* into movement |
| place position prepositions |

Prepositions with the genitive case

A few prepositions are followed by the **genitive case**.

Trotz des schlechten Wetters ...
Despite the bad weather ...

Während der Pause ...
During break ...

1 Complete the list of prepositions followed by the genitive case.

außerhalb	outside
statt	_____ of
trotz	_____
_____	during
wegen	_____ of

2 Translate the sentences into English.

a Wegen des Regens können wir keinen Sport machen.

_____

b Statt unserer Lehrerin hat uns der Direktor in Deutsch unterrichtet.

_____

c Während der Fete waren meine Eltern bei Nachbarn.

_____

d Wir wohnen etwa fünf Kilometer außerhalb der Stadt.

_____

e Während der Wanderung fing es an zu schneien.

_____

f Trotz ihrer Erkältung ist sie schwimmen gegangen.

_____

3 Sort the prepositions into the appropriate boxes in the table.

> an auf aus außer außerhalb bei
> durch entlang für gegen gegenüber
> hinter in mit nach neben ohne seit
> statt trotz über um unter von
> vor während wegen wider zu zwischen

Accusative only	Dative only

Accusative or dative	Genitive

Verbs with prepositions

Some verbs are commonly used with prepositions. These are often different from English. If there is a choice of accusative or dative, most use the accusative case.

Be careful with a few verbs that take a preposition in English but do not in German, e.g. *suchen* (to look <u>for</u>), *hören* (to listen <u>to</u>).

1 Match the pairs.

1	to look forward to	**a**	auskommen mit (+ D)
2	to wait for	**b**	halten von (+ D)
3	to talk about	**c**	sich freuen auf (+ A)
4	to get on with	**d**	sparen auf (+ A)
5	to be interested in	**e**	warten auf (+ A)
6	to taste of	**f**	sprechen über (+ A)
7	to think of (have an opinion of)	**g**	schmecken nach (+ D)
		h	sich interessieren für (+ A)
8	to save for		

2 Complete sentences a–h as indicated in the brackets. Complete sentences i–l with your own choice.

a Sie kommt gut _____ (*with her*) Eltern aus.

b Mein Bruder spart _____ (*for a*) neues Rad.

c Ich warte schon seit 30 Minuten _____ (*for the*) Bus!

d Interessierst du dich _____ (*in classical*) Musik?

e Was hältst du _____ (*of our*) neuen Direktor?

f Igitt! Diese Bonbons schmecken _____ (*of*) Fisch!

g Wir freuen uns _____ (*to the*) Sommerferien.

h Ich muss zehn Minuten lang _____ (*about my*) Hobbys sprechen.

i Ich spare _____.

j Ich komme gut _____ aus.

k Ich interessiere mich _____.

l Ich freue mich _____.

3 Translate these phrases into German. Think carefully about the case to use.

a during the lunch break _____

b out of the house _____

c (throw it) under the chair _____

d at the Schmidt's house _____

e from my uncle _____

f along the street _____

g through the park _____

h after one week _____

i for his aunt _____

j into the baker's _____

k round the corner _____

l for a month _____

m (hang it) on the wall _____

n (drive up) in front of the house _____

o because of his teacher _____

p (it is) on the cupboard _____

q without her money _____

r (put it) behind the door _____

s despite the price _____

t instead of a present _____

u opposite the hotel _____

v (it is) next to the church _____

w except for the children _____

x outside the sports centre _____

y (sit down) between the tables _____

z (it flew) over the house _____

aa with my grandparents _____

ab to the supermarket _____

ac into the theatre _____

ad against a tree _____

Adjectives

What is an adjective?

1 Underline the adjectives in the following passage. You don't need to understand every word, but you should be able to say whether it is an adjective or not.

Das südwestafrikanische Namibia ist ein schönes Land, aber es gibt dort große Kontraste. Windhoek, die ziemlich moderne Hauptstadt, hat riesige Wohnblocks, tolle Einkaufszentren, breite Straßen mit lauten Autos. Auf dem Land aber sind viele Menschen sehr arm. Sie wohnen in primitiven Hütten ohne moderne Annehmlichkeiten wie Elektrizität und Wasser. Es gibt viel Wüste, wo das Leben sehr hart ist. Es gibt aber auch eine lange Küste am Atlantik. Dort kann man verschiedene Wassersportarten betreiben. Ausländische Touristen besuchen Namibia, um die imposante Landschaft zu sehen und die schönen afrikanischen Tiere zu fotografieren.

2 Fill in as many German adjectives as you can on the spider diagram and give their English translation. If the space isn't big enough, do this on a separate piece of paper.

Adjectives used after a noun

3 Choose an adjective from the box to fill each gap. Be careful – some adjectives in the box have endings on them.

a Mein Meerschweinchen ist sehr _____ .

b Alle Lehrer sind _____ .

c Nach der Schule bin ich immer _____ .

d Unser Haus ist _____ , aber _____ .

e Meine Weihnachtsgeschenke waren sehr

_____ .

f Das Feuerwerk an Sylvester war _____ .

alt altes bequem bequeme intelligent intelligenten müde müden süß süße teuer wunderbar

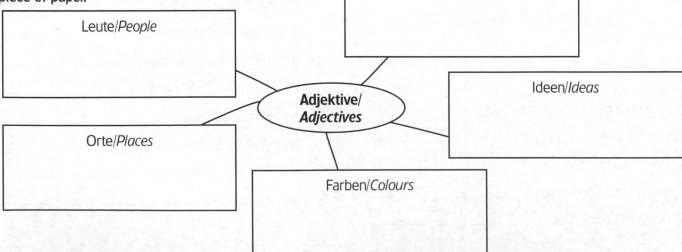

Leute/*People*

Orte/*Places*

Anderes/*Other*

Ideen/*Ideas*

Adjektive/ *Adjectives*

Farben/*Colours*

Adjectives with the definite article

These are the adjectival endings with the definite article:

	Masculine	Feminine	Neuter	Plural
Nominative	der alte Hund	die alte Katze	das alte Pferd	die alten Tiere
Accusative	den alten Hund	die alte Katze	das alte Pferd	die alten Tiere
Genitive	des alten Hundes	der alten Katze	des alten Pferdes	der alten Tiere
Dative	dem alten Hund	der alten Katze	dem alten Pferd	den alten Tieren

There are only two different endings — most are -en and the rest are -e.

The same pattern applies with these determiners: *dieser, jener, jeder, welcher*.

1 Look at the gender/number and case of the underlined noun phrases and choose the correct description for each from the box.

a Was kostet die neue CD von dieser Gruppe?

_____

b Der junge Mann erklärt dir alles.

_____

c Die Musik ist viel besser durch die teuren Kopfhörer.

_____

d Was ist der Preis des kleinen Radios dort?

_____

e Was soll ich mit dem alten CD-Spieler machen?

_____

f Ich kaufe mir die tolle Sammlung von Tanzmusik.

_____

```
masculine/nominative    plural/accusative
masculine/dative    feminine/accusative
feminine/nominative    neuter/genitive
```

2 Now describe the gender and case of each underlined noun phrase.

a Wie findest du den politischen Dokumentarfilm?

_____

b Alles in der neuen Serie ist sehr interessant.

_____

c Siehst du oft die Sendungen des Zweiten Programms?

_____

d Die letzte Sendung beginnt um wie viel Uhr?

_____

e Habt ihr gestern das blöde Quiz gesehen?

_____

f Wann sind die Nachrichten im Ersten Programm?

_____

3 Underline the correct adjective in each sentence.

a Der (deutsche/deutscher) Autor Günter Grass hat den Nobelpreis gewonnen.

b Ich bin mit der (neunte/neunten) Klasse ins Theater gegangen.

c Hast du diesen (interessanten/interessantem) Film über Hamburg gesehen?

d Ich sehe oft Filme auf *Arte*, aber die (anderes/anderen) Kanäle sehe ich wenig.

e Mit jedem (neuen/neuer) Krimi sieht man mehr Realismus.

f Das (deutsche/deutschen) Fernsehen ist nicht schlecht.

4 Add the correct ending to each adjective.

a Die jung_____ Frau Krohn hat schon vier Kinder.

b Markus ist der einzig_____ Sohn.

c Die ander_____ Kinder sind alle Mädchen.

d Die Kinder spielen oft mit den stolz_____ Großeltern.

e Es ist manchmal schwierig in diesem klein_____ Haus.

f Für den jung_____ Vater ist es auch nicht leicht.

Adjectives with the indefinite article

TIPP

These are the adjectival endings with the indefinite article (and the negative):

	Masculine	Feminine	Neuter	Plural
Nominative	ein alt**er** Hund	eine alt**e** Katze	ein alt**es** Pferd	keine alt**en** Tiere
Accusative	einen alt**en** Hund	eine alt**e** Katze	ein alt**es** Pferd	keine alt**en** Tiere
Genitive	eines alt**en** Hundes	einer alt**en** Katze	eines alt**en** Pferdes	keiner alt**en** Tiere
Dative	einem alt**en** Hund	einer alt**en** Katze	einem alt**en** Pferd	keinen alt**en** Tieren

There are only three changes from the definite article pattern (masculine nominative; neuter nominative and accusative).

The same pattern applies with all the possessive adjectives: *mein, dein, sein* etc.

---

1 Choose an adjective from the box to complete each sentence.

a Mein Onkel ist ein _____ Geschäftsmann.

b Er hat ein _____ Schuhgeschäft in der Stadtmitte.

c Ich kaufe immer meine _____ Schuhe bei ihm.

d Obwohl er reich ist, hat er eine total _____ Familie.

e Ich komme gut mit seiner _____ Tochter aus.

f Ich habe keine _____ Cousins.

g Seine _____ Frau arbeitet auch in der Firma.

h Aber ihr _____ Hund arbeitet natürlich nicht!

> anderen   brauner   elegante   großes
> guter   jüngeren   neuen   normale

2 Add the correct ending to each adjective.

a Meine Familie hat einen neu_____ Hund.

b Unsere schön_____ Katzen sind nicht froh darüber!

c Früher hatten wir kein groß_____ Haus und keine Haustiere.

d Jetzt aber wohnen wir auf einem alt_____ Bauernhof mit einem groß_____ Garten.

e Das Haus ist am Rande eines hübsch_____ Dorfs.

f Es gibt einen klein_____ Supermarkt und eine langweilig_____ Kneipe.

g Wir haben keine interessant_____ Vereine.

h Manchmal fahre ich mit einer freundlich_____ Nachbarin in die Stadt.

3 Complete Anja and Laura's conversation with the correct adjective endings. Look at the determiner to decide which ending to use. Remember – some adjectives don't need an extra ending.

A: Katrin gibt eine groß_____ Party und ich brauche einen neu_____ Rock.

L: Ja, sie lädt die ganz_____ Klasse ein und ich gehe auch mit meinem neu_____ Freund hin.

A: Der ist so süß_____! Was trägst du zu dieser toll_____ Party?

L: Ich trage meine neu_____ Jeans, aber ich möchte ein neu_____ T-Shirt.

A: Siehst du das grün_____ T-Shirt dort drüben?

L: Schick! Ich habe kein gut_____ T-Shirt. Und du, siehst du diesen blau_____ Rock?

A: Der Rock ist schön_____, aber die hässlich_____ Farbe gefällt mir nicht. Und der Preis dieses schwarz_____ Rocks ist viel zu hoch_____.

L: Gehen wir in ein ander_____ Geschäft. Welche modern_____ Modegeschäfte gibt es hier?

A: Es gibt die groß_____ Kaufhäuser. Sie haben bestimmt einen billig_____ Rock für mich.

L: Also, wir gehen in einen billig_____ Laden und kaufen uns die perfekt_____ Kleidung für eine wichtig_____ Party!

Adjectives with no determiner

Sometimes an adjective has **no determiner** but is used by itself with a noun ('black coffee', 'good food' etc.). The adjective then takes the endings that the definite article would have had (with slight changes in the neuter and the genitive):

	Masculine	Feminine	Neuter	Plural
Nominative	hart**er** Käse	warm**e** Milch	kalt**es** Wasser	heiß**e** Würste
Accusative	hart**en** Käse	warm**e** Milch	kalt**es** Wasser	heiß**e** Würste
Genitive	hart**en** Käses	warm**er** Milch	kalt**en** Wassers	heiß**er** Würste
Dative	hart**em** Käse	warm**er** Milch	kalt**em** Wasser	heiß**en** Würsten

These endings are also used after numbers and some plural words like *viele*, *wenige* and *einige*.

1 Underline the adjectival phrases and write down their gender (m, f, n), number (sing., pl.) and case (N, A, G, D). Some sentences have more than one phrase associated with them.

a Ich höre sehr gern <u>kreative Musik</u>. **e.g.** *f. sing., A*

b Laute Musik kann gefährlich sein. _____

c Mit guten Noten hat man kaum große Probleme. _____

d Es soll gesund sein, in kaltem Wasser zu baden. _____

e Ich habe zwei süße Katzen. _____

f Das Mittelmeer hat viele goldene Strände. _____

g Die Farbe einiger neuer Autos finde ich furchtbar. _____

h Meine Schwester bekommt tolle Geschenke. _____

2 Add the correct adjectival endings.

a Ich höre nicht so gern deutsch_____ Musik.

b Ich finde sie schlechter als englisch_____ Musik.

c *Gut_____ Zeiten, schlecht_____ Zeiten* ist eine Fernsehserie.

d Mein Vater trinkt nur schwarz_____ Kaffee und grün_____ Tee.

e Frisch_____ warm_____ Brot schmeckt sagenhaft!

f Mit gut_____ Freunden kann man schön_____ Abende verbringen.

g Ich habe mit drei interessant_____ Damen gesprochen.

h Im Sommer brauche ich heiß_____ Wetter und teur_____ Hotels.

3 Complete the tables of the three groups of endings.

der/dieser/jener/jeder/welcher	Masculine	Feminine	Neuter	Plural
N	–e			–en
A				
G				
D				

ein/kein/mein/dein/sein/ihr/unser/euer	Masculine	Feminine	Neuter	Plural
N	–e			–en
A				
G				
D				

No determiner	Masculine	Feminine	Neuter	Plural
N	–er			
A				
G			–en	
D				

Adjectives used as nouns

1 Match the pairs.

1	etwas Gutes	**a**	nothing English
2	nichts Besonderes	**b**	because of a lot of new stuff
3	wegen viel Neuem	**c**	for nothing boring
4	von wenig Interessantem	**d**	little that's important
5	statt etwas Teurem	**e**	something good
6	aus etwas Altem	**f**	a lot of green
7	nichts Englisches	**g**	instead of something expensive
8	mit viel Billigem	**h**	something sharp
9	etwas Scharfes	**i**	nothing special
10	für nichts Langweiliges	**j**	out of something old
11	viel Grünes	**k**	of little of interest
12	wenig Wichtiges	**l**	with a lot of cheap stuff

TIPP

After words such as *wenig* (little), *etwas* (something), *viel* (a lot) and *nichts* (nothing) you can use **adjectives as nouns** – just add a capital letter and the neuter endings from 'adjectives with no determiner' (page 23).

Nominative	etwas Gut**es**
Accusative	nichts Besonder**es**
Genitive	viel Neu**en**
Dative	wenig Interessant**em**

2 Translate these phrases into German.

a something blue _____

b with a lot of good stuff _____

c nothing important _____

d little that's special _____

e on something cold
(*auf* + dative) _____

f nothing hot _____

TIPP

You can also use **adjectives as nouns** after *alles* (all, everything), but this changes in a different way – *alles* behaves like *das* (neuter definite article) and you add a capital letter and the correct endings to the adjective.

Nominative	alles Gut**e**
Accusative	alles Gut**e**
Genitive	alles Gut**en**
Dative	allem Gut**en**

3 Choose four of the German phrases from Exercise 1 and put them in a full sentence:

e.g. *In Irland gibt es viel Grünes.*

a _____
_____

b _____
_____

c _____
_____

d _____
_____

4 Complete the sentences with the correct form of the adjective in brackets.

a Er wünschte mir alles _____. (gut)

b Sie haben uns alles _____ angeboten. (möglich)

c Sie hat alles _____ in die Waschmaschine gesteckt. (schmutzig)

d Wir haben alles _____ gegessen. (gesund)

Comparative adjectives

1 Complete the table. Fill in four adjectives of your own choice at the end.

Adjective	Meaning	Comparative	Meaning
schön	*beautiful*	schöner	*more beautiful*
		älter	*older*
		jünger	
	cold		
arm			*poorer*
		wärmer	
		länger	
intelligent			
wichtig			*more important*
		fauler	
aktiv			
durstig			
		hungriger	
billig			
		teurer	
	healthy	gesünder	
			more dangerous
hoch			*higher*
	good	besser	

2 Change the adjectives in brackets to the comparative form. Remember to keep the adjectival ending, if there is one.

a Diese Straße ist (lang) _____.

b In den Geschäften hat man eine (gute) _____ Auswahl.

c Dieser Wohnblock ist (hoch) _____.

d Ein (alter) _____ Mann wohnt im zehnten Stock.

e Das Geschenk ist für ein (freundliches) _____ Mädchen.

f Frau Bolle will mit (jungen) _____ Leuten arbeiten.

3 Change the adjectives in brackets to the comparative form and add the correct adjectival endings. Look for the determiner (or lack of one) to decide which endings to use.

a Viele Leute treiben Sport, um (fit) _____ zu werden.

b Sport spielt heute eine (wichtig) _____ Rolle im Leben vieler Deutschen als vor 20 Jahren.

c Es gibt auch (interessant) _____ Sportarten als früher.

d In einer (groß) _____ Sporthalle sieht man viele Sportarten auf einmal.

e Weniger Deutsche als Engländer spielen Golf, vielleicht weil es in Deutschland (teuer) _____ ist.

4 Write full sentences as suggested by the prompts:

\> means 'more ... than'

= means 'just as ...'

≠ means 'not as ...'

e.g. Fernsehen > Musik (interessant)

→ *Fernsehen ist interessanter als Musik.*

You can compare two things by saying:

X ist größ**er als** Y	bigg**er than**
X ist **nicht so** groß **wie** Y	**not as** big **as**
X ist **genauso** groß **wie** Y	**just as** big **as**

a Schokolade ≠ Obst (gesund) _____ .

b Markus = Andreas (schlank) _____ .

c Anja > Eva (faul) _____ .

d ich > mein Bruder (jung) _____ .

e meine Mutter ≠ mein Vater (alt) _____ .

f Bücher > Filme (gut) _____ .

g das T-Shirt = das Hemd (teuer) _____ .

h der Frühling ≠ der Winter (kalt) _____ .

i Süßigkeiten > Hamburger (schlecht) _____ .

Superlative adjectives

Use **superlative adjectives** to compare three or more things and say which is 'the long**est**', 'the **most** interesting' etc. In German, just add *-st* or *-est* to an adjective, e.g. *läng**st*** or *interessant**est***.

Some short adjectives add an Umlaut in the same way as the comparatives can. And, of course, there are a few common irregular superlatives:

gut – besser – best	*nah – näher – nächst*
hoch – höher – höchst	

As with all adjectives, a superlative adjective adds the usual endings when used with a noun (see pages 21–23):

*die best**e** Wahl   mein best**er** Freund*

*im neuest**en** Buch*

1 Translate into English.

a unser bester Lehrer _____

b das billigste Geschäft _____

c die schönsten Farben _____

d im interessantesten Film _____

e für sein ältestes Kind _____

2 Choose a word from the box to complete each sentence.

a Das schnellste Auto ist auch das _____ .

b Die Schüler mit den besten Noten sind oft die _____ .

c Der billigste Kuli ist nicht immer der _____ .

d Alte Leute sind in vielen Ländern die _____ .

e Meiner Meinung nach ist diese Sendung die _____ .

ärmsten	beste	fleißigsten
schlechteste	teuerste	

3 Translate into German.

a the poorest people _____

b in the longest film _____

c after the worst exam _____

d the nearest town _____

e Peter is my eldest cousin _____

Adverbs

What is an adverb?

Adverbs tell you more about a verb – they describe when, how or where something happened. They can be one word (*schnell, pünktlich*) or they can be whole adverbial phrases (*um 7 Uhr, mit dem Bus*).

Most German adverbs look exactly the same as an adjective and they do not add any endings:

> *Sie ist eine **fleißig**e Schülerin.*
> She's a hard–working student. (adjective)

> *Sie arbeitet **fleißig**.*
> She works hard. (adverb)

> *Das Spiel war **gut**.*
> The game was good. (adjective)

> *Wir haben **gut** gespielt.*
> We played well. (adverb)

1 Underline the adverbs and adverbial phrases and put a translation for them in the brackets.

a Monika lernt für die Prüfungen, aber sie macht regelmäßig Pausen.

(_____)

b Sie lernt besser, wenn sie Musik hört.

(_____)

c Ihre Brüder essen immer gesund.

(_____)

d Abends kann ich mich nicht so gut konzentrieren.

(_____)

e Auf der Autobahn fährt man oft zu schnell.

(_____)

f Ich will nicht arbeiten – ich möchte in Ruhe lesen.

(_____)

g Ich werde mich warm anziehen, weil es kalt ist.

(_____)

h Wir warten nervös auf den Direktor.

(_____)

2 Look at your answers for Exercise 1 and complete this sentence.

The ending -____ in English is often used for adverbs.

Comparative and superlative adverbs

Comparative and superlative adverbs are formed in the same way as for adjectives. There are also the same few irregular ones.

Examples of adverbs	Comparative: add -er	Superlative: put *am* in front of the adverb and add -(e)sten to it
schlecht (badly)	*schlechter* (worse)	**am** *schlecht**esten*** (the worst)
gut (well)	*besser* (better)	*am besten* (the best)
viel (a lot)	*mehr* (more)	*am meisten* (the most)

3 Complete the comparisons as in the example. On separate paper translate each sentence into English and make up a similar one of your own:

e.g. Paul arbeitet <u>schnell</u>, Anja arbeitet <u>schneller</u>, aber Alex arbeitet <u>am schnellsten</u>. *Paul works quickly, Anja works more quickly, but Alex works most quickly.*

a Waschmittel A wäscht alles sauber, B wäscht alles _____, aber C wäscht alles am _____

b Mein Vater fährt _____, aber meine Mutter fährt vorsichtiger und meine Oma fährt _____ .

c Ich schwimme _____, ich jogge mehr, und _____ fahre ich Rad.

d Bananen schmecken _____ , Orangen schmecken _____ , aber Äpfel schmecken am besten.

4 Complete the sentences, following the prompts.

a Wo dürfen wir unsere Musik (*the loudest*) _____ spielen?

b Ich glaube, deutsche Züge kommen (*the most punctually*) _____ an.

c Wer kann (*the highest*) _____ springen?

d Sara kann (*the longest*) _____ unter Wasser schwimmen.

Liking and preferring

TIPP

Liking and preferring can be difficult to translate into German. These adverbs are very useful:

gern (indicates **liking** and goes after the verb) *nicht gern* (indicates **not liking**)	*lieber* (indicates **preferring** and goes after the verb)	*am liebsten* (shows what you **most like** and also goes after the verb, but may also be used at the beginning of the sentence or clause for emphasis)

Ich trinke gern Wasser, aber ich trinke lieber Saft. Am liebsten trinke ich Limonade.
I like drinking water, but I prefer juice. I like lemonade most of all.

The verb is very important – the adverbs just add more information, telling you **how much** someone likes **doing** something.

Er singt. Er singt gern/lieber/am liebsten.

1 **Read the sentences and complete the table.**

a Ich esse gern Obst, aber ich esse lieber Kekse.

b Sport ist toll – am liebsten schwimme ich.

c Ich spiele gern Geige im Orchester.

d Ich lese lieber Fantasie-Romane.

e Obst und Kekse sind nicht schlecht, aber am liebsten esse ich Schokolade.

f Ich spiele nicht gern Tennis – ich mache lieber Leichtathletik.

g Das ist blöd, aber am liebsten sehe ich fern.

Put the items in order from 1 (most liked) to 3 (least liked).

	Food	Sport	Other activities
1			
2			
3			

2 **Translate the following sentences into German.**

a I like eating bread.

_____ .

b He prefers playing football.

_____ .

c She likes listening to music most of all.

_____ .

d We like learning German.

_____ .

e They don't like watching TV.

_____ .

f Do you prefer (to drink) tea or coffee?

_____ .

TIPP

There are other ways of expressing likes and dislikes.

Infinitive	Present	Imperfect	Perfect
mögen	ich mag ...	ich mochte ...	ich habe ... gemocht
gefallen	mir gefällt ... (singular)	mir gefiel ... (singular)	... hat mir gefallen
	mir gefallen ... (plural)	mir gefielen ... (plural)	... haben mir gefallen

Remember that *gefallen* is used with the dative case (see page 7).

See the Verbs section for more about tenses.

3 **Match the pairs. Write a–f in the boxes.**

1 Als Kind mochte ich viele Cartoons. ☐

2 Magst du klassische Musik? ☐

3 Gefällt dir diese Filmmusik? ☐

4 Mir haben Tintin-Bücher immer gefallen. ☐

5 Cartoons gefallen mir sehr. ☐

6 Ich habe Tintin nie gemocht. ☐

a Do you like this film music?

b As a child I liked a lot of cartoons.

c I really like cartoons.

d I've never liked Tintin.

e Do you like classical music?

f I've always liked Tintin books.

Interrogative adverbs

TIPP

Some **question words** are adverbs (**interrogative adverbs**) and some are pronouns (**interrogative pronouns** – see page 35). These 'w' words are placed at the beginning of a sentence to make it into a question. Remember to put the verb next (see page 38).

1 Complete the list of question words and their meaning.

wann	_____
wie	how
wo	_____
warum	why
wie viel(e) ...	how much (how _____) ...
was	_____
_____ *(wen, wem)*	who (whom)
was für ...	what _____ of ...

many	sort	*wer*	what	when	where

2 Insert the correct question words.

a _____ beginnt die erste Stunde?

b _____ hast du in der Stadt gekauft?

c _____ ein Buch liest du da?

d _____ Geld hast du?

e _____ treffen wir uns heute Abend?

f _____ spielst du deine Musik so laut?

was für	wann	warum	was	wie viel	wo

3 Write the questions that could give these answers. Remember, most of the information you need for the question is provided in the answer.

a _____
_____?

Ich fahre um 18 Uhr nach Hause.

b _____
_____?

Ich lese dieses Buch, weil es sehr lustig ist.

c _____
_____?

Ich habe tausend Briefmarken.

d _____
_____?

Thomas spielt Fußball.

e _____
_____?

Er spielt im Park Fußball.

f _____
_____?

Ich fahre mit dem Bus oder mit dem Rad zur Schule.

4 Write a complete question of your choice for each of these question words.

a Wer _____?

b Was _____?

c Wann _____?

d Wo _____?

e Warum _____?

f Wie _____?

g Wie viele _____?

h Was für _____?

Adverbial phrases of time and place

1 Complete the list. Use a dictionary if necessary.

(Time)

manchmal	_____
immer	always
_____	often
nie	never
ab und zu	now and again
dann und wann	now and then
so bald wie möglich	as _____ as possible
nächste Woche	next _____
nächstes Wochenende	_____
nächsten _____	next Monday
letztes Jahr	last year
letzte _____	last week
letzten _____	last Tuesday
nach der Schule	after _____
vor dem Frühstück	_____ breakfast
vor drei Jahren	_____ years ago
vor zwei Monaten	two _____ ago
jeden _____	every day
sonntags	every _____, on Sundays
um 8 Uhr	at 8 o'clock
im Sommer	in the _____

(Manner)

mit dem Bus	by bus
mit Freunden	with _____
mit meiner _____	with my family

(Place)

hier	_____
dort	there
in der Stadt	in town
in die Stadt	into _____
nach Berlin	to Berlin
zum Supermarkt	_____ the supermarket

2 Use the list to help you translate these phrases into German.

a last weekend _____

b every Monday _____

c one month ago _____

d next year _____

e to Freiburg _____

f with a friend _____

3 Rearrange the adverbial phrases (underlined in the following) to give the correct word order.

a Ich fahre <u>nach München</u> <u>mit der Klasse</u> <u>morgen</u>.

Ich _____.

b Man kann <u>am Fluss</u> <u>sonntags</u> <u>mit dem Hund</u> spazieren gehen.

Man kann _____

_____ spazieren gehen.

c Viele junge Deutsche verbringen <u>in England</u> ein Jahr <u>als Au-Pair</u>.

Viele _____

_____.

Intensifiers

1 Complete this list of intensifiers. Use a dictionary if necessary.

ein bisschen	a _____
ein wenig	a little
einfach	simply
ganz	quite, completely
gar nicht	_____ at all
kaum	hardly
sehr	_____
so	so
total	totally
überhaupt _____	not at all
viel (+ comparative)	much more ...
ziemlich	_____, fairly
zu	too

2 Fill each gap with a suitable intensifier and translate the sentences into English.

a Unsere Deutschlehrerin ist _____ intelligent.

_____.

b Meine Freundin hat _____ fleißig gearbeitet.

_____.

c Du bist ein _____ sportlicher Junge.

_____.

d Wir haben gestern _____ gut gespielt.

_____.

e Gemüse esse ich _____ gern.

_____.

f Vegetarier sind _____ interessanter als andere Menschen!

_____.

3 Complete this summary of adverbs. Use the words in the box.

Adverbs tell you more about when, how and where the action of a (1) _____ happens.

They can be (2) _____ word, or they can be a whole adverbial (3) _____ .

Most German adverbs look exactly the same as an (4) _____ .

Adverbs do not add any (5) _____ .

Comparative and (6) _____ adverbs are formed in the same way as for adjectives.

Many (7) _____ words are adverbs and they all begin with 'w'.

Adverbs and adverbial phrases must go in this order in a sentence: (8) _____ – manner – place.

Intensifiers are used to add (9) _____ to a word or phrase.

verb	time	endings	one	phrase	emphasis
	superlative	question	adjective		

4 Write down as many adverbs as you can think of in German.

_____	_____
_____	_____
_____	_____
_____	_____
_____	_____
_____	_____
_____	_____
_____	_____
_____	_____

Pronouns

What is a pronoun?

A **pronoun** is a short word that replaces a noun (or noun phrase) to avoid repetition. Like nouns, pronouns change their case depending on the part they play in a sentence.

Here are the **personal pronouns** in the most common cases:

Nominative	Accusative	Dative	
ich	mich	mir	I, me
du	dich	dir	you
er	ihn	ihm	he/it, him
sie	sie	ihr	she/it, her
es	es	ihm	it
wir	uns	uns	we, us
ihr	euch	euch	you (familiar plural)
Sie	Sie	Ihnen	you (polite)
sie	sie	ihnen	they, them

Sie hat **mich** gesehen.
She saw **me**.

*Anja und Thomas, kommt **ihr** mit **uns** ins Kino?*
Anja und Thomas, are **you** coming to the cinema with **us**?

1 Underline the pronouns. Write down what case they are and why:

e.g. Diana kennt Ibrahim schon. <u>Sie</u> hat <u>mich</u> mit <u>ihm</u> gesehen:

<u>sie</u> = nominative, subject of the verb (has seen)

<u>mich</u> = accusative, direct object of the verb (has seen)

<u>ihm</u> = dative, with preposition **mit**

a Die Lehrerin hat ein neues Heft für mich.

_____.

_____.

b Die Arbeit ist zu schwer. Wir können sie nicht machen.

_____.

_____.

c Ich liebe meine Oma und verbringe oft ein Wochenende bei ihr.

_____.

_____.

d Wollt ihr auf meinem Computer spielen? Er ist wirklich toll!

_____.

_____.

e Da sind Paul und Ines. Sie fahren mit mir in die Stadt.

_____.

_____.

f Sie sind ohne mich losgefahren!

_____.

_____.

2 Fill the gaps with the correct form of *ich* or *du*.

a Kannst du _____ hören?

b Ich kann _____ nicht sehen.

c Gib _____ deine Hand.

d Soll ich _____ die Butter reichen?

e Was möchtest _____ als Nachtisch?

3 Fill the gaps with the correct form of *wir*, *ihr*, *Sie* or *sie*.

a Laura und Leon sind Kinder − _____ sprechen mit ihrem Vater:

b Vati, gib _____ bitte 5 Euro.

c Ich habe _____ schon gesagt − nein!

d Aber _____ wollen einen Comic kaufen.

e _____ lest zu viele blöde Comics.

f Ja, aber _____ sind lustig.

Personal pronouns

The pronouns *er*, *ihn* and *ihm* refer to any masculine noun, not just a male person, so they can sometimes mean 'it' rather than 'he' or 'him'.

Similarly *sie* and *ihr* are for any feminine noun, and *es* and *ihm* for any neuter noun. For example, the pronoun for *der* Bus is *er* (it); the pronoun for *die* Jacke is *sie* (it); the pronoun for *das* Mädchen is *es* (she).

1 Fill the gaps with the correct form of *er*, *sie* or *es*.

a Ich verstehe mich gut mit _____ (*her*).

b Ich sehe _____ (*him*) jeden Tag.

c Das ist mein Buch. _____ (*it*) ist sehr interessant.

d Wo ist meine Jacke? Ich finde _____ (*it*) nicht.

e Der Zug hat Verspätung. _____ (*it*) kommt in 10 Minuten an.

f Ich habe meinen Kuli verloren. Hast du _____ (*it*) gesehen?

You will often find the dative pronouns after verbs such as *geben*, *sagen*, *erzählen* and *zeigen*.

Some verbs that are always followed by the dative are *passen*, *helfen* and *gefallen*. (See also page 7.)

*Ich sage **dir** die Wahrheit.*
I'm telling **you** the truth.

*Das Buch gefällt **mir**.*
I like the book. ('The book pleases me.')

*Sie hilft **ihm** bei der Arbeit.*
She helps **him** with his work.

*Das Kleid passt **ihr** nicht.*
The dress doesn't fit/suit **her**.

2 Fill in the gap with the correct dative pronoun.

a Wir helfen _____ (*them*) bei der Arbeit.

b Diese Schuhe gefallen _____ (*her*) sehr.

c Warte mal, Erika, ich sage _____ (*you*) die Antwort.

d Unsere Schuluniform gefällt _____ (*us*) überhaupt nicht.

e Ich habe _____ (*him*) meine Hausaufgaben gegeben.

f Nein, Mutti, deine Jacke passt _____ (*me*) überhaupt nicht.

g Herr Krohn, ich möchte _____ (*you*) meine Arbeit zeigen.

h Also, Kinder, ich erzähle _____ (*you*) eine tolle Geschichte.

3 Fill in the gap with the correct pronoun. There is a mixture of all the pronouns and cases.

a Was ist mit _____ (*you*) los?

b Otto hat einen neue Freundin. _____ (*she*) ist nicht sehr nett.

c _____ (*He*) hat _____ (*her*) eine Halskette gegeben.

d I last _____ (*you*) etwas für _____ (*me*)?

e Kannst du _____ (*me*) einen Witz erzählen?

f Bastian? Ich finde _____ (*him*) sehr sympathisch.

g Wie war die Sendung? Ich habe _____ (*it*) nicht gesehen.

h Frau Herbert, ich möchte mit _____ (*you*) sprechen.

i Da fährt der Bus – ich habe _____ (*it*) verpasst.

j Meine Oma wohnt zur Zeit bei _____ (*us*).

Reflexive pronouns

Reflexive pronouns are used with reflexive verbs (see page 43). They usually mean 'myself', yourself' etc. and they are used in the accusative and dative cases.

Subject (nominative)	Reflexive pronouns		Meaning
	accusative	dative	
ich	mich	mir	myself
du	dich	dir	yourself
er, sie, es	sich	sich	himself, herself, itself
wir	uns	uns	ourselves
ihr	euch	euch	yourselves
Sie	sich	sich	yourself, yourselves
sie	sich	sich	themselves

Most reflexive verbs have the accusative case of a **reflexive pronoun**, e.g. *Ich ziehe **mich** an* − I get dressed (I dress **myself**). This is because *mich* is the direct object of the verb.

1 Fill in the gap with the correct pronoun. These are all in the accusative.

a Ich dusche _____ jeden Morgen.

b Für die Sportstunde ziehen wir _____ natürlich um.

c Thomas und Martin fühlen _____ nicht wohl.

d Thomas legt _____ auf sein Bett.

e Interessieren Sie _____ für Volleyball?

f Meine Schwester zieht _____ immer vor dem Frühstück an.

g Mein Kaninchen freut _____ auf den Salat!

h Das ist besser − ich habe _____ schön ausgeruht.

i Ihr wascht _____ am besten im Badezimmer, nicht in der Küche.

A few reflexive verbs take the dative case (which conveys the idea of 'to someone'), e.g. *Ich putze **mir** die Zähne* − I brush my teeth (I brush 'to me' the teeth). These verbs always have a direct object (in this case, 'teeth').

These common verbs take the dative reflexive pronoun:

sich (etwas) wünschen − to wish (for something) − *Ich wünsche **mir** einen neuen Computer.*

sich (etwas) ansehen − to watch (something) − *Siehst du **dir** den Film an?*

sich (etwas) kaufen − to buy yourself (something) − *Ich kaufe **mir** einen Pullover.*

2 Circle the reflexive pronoun and underline the direct object (accusative) in these sentences containing reflexive verbs. Then translate each sentence.

a Alexander wäscht sich die Hände vor dem Essen.

_____.

b Kaufst du dir eine neue Jeans in der Stadt?

_____.

c Heute Abend sehe ich mir einen alten Film an.

_____.

d Zum Geburtstag wünschst sie sich ein Mountainbike.

_____.

e Hast du dir die Zähne geputzt?

_____.

f Kämm dir bitte die Haare!

_____.

3 Fill in the gap with the correct reflexive pronoun. There is a mixture of accusative and dative.

a Meine Familie interessiert _____ für Sport.

b Ich habe _____ einen Hamburger gekauft.

c Fühlst du _____ jetzt krank?

d Wir haben _____ nach dem Spiel geduscht.

e Habt ihr _____ das Spiel im Fernsehen angesehen?

f Was wünschen Sie _____ zu Weihnachten?

Indefinite pronouns

TIPP

The **indefinite pronouns** are *jemand* (someone) and *niemand* (no one). They usually change to *jemanden/ niemanden* in the accusative and to *jemandem/ niemandem* in the dative.

> *Jemand ist vorbeigegangen, aber ich habe niemanden gesehen und mit niemandem gesprochen.*
> Someone went by, but I saw no one and spoke to no one.

1 Underline the correct indefinite pronoun in each sentence.

a (Niemand/Niemanden) kommt mit ins Kino.

b Hast du (jemanden/jemandem) im Garten gesehen?

c Er ist mit (jemand/jemandem) gekommen, aber ich weiß nicht, wie er heißt.

d Du darfst (niemand/niemandem) sagen, was du gehört hast!

e (Jemand/Jemanden) soll hier bleiben.

Interrogative pronouns

TIPP

As we saw earlier (page 29), some **question words** are adverbs (interrogative adverbs). Others are pronouns (**interrogative pronouns**). Like the interrogative adverbs, these 'w' words are placed at the beginning of a sentence to make it into a question. Remember to put the verb next (see page 38).

The interrogative pronoun *wer* changes to *wen* in the accusative and to *wem* in the dative.

> ***Wer** kommt mit?* – Who is coming with us?
> ***Wen** hast du gesehen?* – Who(m) did you see?
> *Mit **wem** hast du gesprochen?* – With whom did you speak? Who did you speak to?

2 Write the correct interrogative pronoun (*wer, wen, wem*) in the gaps.

a Für _____ ist das Geschenk?

b _____ hat die besten Noten?

c _____ hilfst du nach der Schule? (*helfen + dative*)

d _____ hast du in der Stadt gesehen?

e _____ hat eine Frage?

f Von _____ ist diese E-Mail?

Relative pronouns

TIPP

Relative pronouns are one way of joining two related sentences together. They mean 'that/which' or 'who(m)'.

3 Draw lines to match the sentence halves.

1 Der Lehrer, der
2 Die Frau, die
3 Das Rad, das
4 Die Leute, die
5 Das ist der Bäcker,
6 Das ist die Sendung,
7 Das ist das Café,
8 Das sind die Bücher,

a in der Garage ist, gehört mir.
b das sehr teuer ist.
c Deutsch unterrichtet, ist cool.
d die total blöd ist.
e der mir das Brot verkauft hat.
f ein rotes Kleid trägt, ist meine Mutter.
g die ich eben gekauft habe.
h dort stehen, sind sehr reich.

TIPP

Relative pronouns have to be the same gender, number and case as the noun they replace. Apart from the dative plural, they look just like the words for 'the'.

4 Complete the table.

	Masculine	Feminine	Neuter	Plural
Nom		die		die
Acc	den		das	
Dat		der	dem	denen

5 Join each pair of sentences to make one longer one.

e.g. <u>Dieser Lehrer</u> **ist** cool.
+ <u>Dieser Lehrer</u> **gibt** uns keine Hausaufgaben.
= *Dieser Lehrer, der uns keine Hausaufgaben **gibt**, ist cool.*

a Basketball* gefällt mir sehr. (*masc.)
+ Basketball ist ein Sport für junge Leute.

= _____ .

b Meine beste Lehrerin unterrichtet Physik.
+ Meine Lehrerin heißt Frau Ohm.

= _____ .

c Das blaue Rad kostet € 1000.
+ Das Rad steht vorne im Sportgeschäft.

= _____ .

d Die Olympischen Spiele sind sehr interessant.
+ Die Olympischen Spiele finden alle vier Jahre statt.

= _____ .

6 Which case would you need to translate each of the underlined words into German? Write **N, A or D**:

e.g. The teacher <u>whom</u> I saw.   _A_

a The ski instructor <u>who</u> taught me.   _____

b The tourists with <u>whom</u> we travelled ...   _____

c The cup <u>which</u> she won at the games.   _____

d The book <u>that</u> I am reading.   _____

e The game <u>that</u> is on TV tonight   _____

f The boy for <u>whom</u> I bought this cake.   _____

7 Choose a phrase from the box to complete each sentence. Then, on separate paper, translate each sentence into English.

e.g. Ein Schüler, _3_, bekommt oft schlechte Noten.

a Die jungen Leute, _____, studieren Fremdsprachen.

b Die Dame, _____, war sehr nett.

c Das Mädchen, _____, kann sehr gut Deutsch.

d Der Computer, _____, ist jetzt kaputt.

1 auf dem wir gestern gespielt haben
2 das neben mir sitzt
3 der nicht sehr fleißig arbeitet
4 die mir €20 gegeben hat
5 mit denen ich gesprochen habe

8 Complete the sentences with the correct relative pronoun.

a Die Deutschen, _____ Urlaub im Ausland machen, fahren oft nach Spanien.

b Der Freund, mit _____ ich ins Theater gehe, kommt um 18 Uhr.

c Das Buch, _____ ich im Moment lese, ist ziemlich langweilig.

d Die Strände, an _____ wir uns sonnen, sind so schön.

e Handball ist eine Sportart, _____ in Deutschland sehr populär ist.

f Die Sporthalle, in _____ wir spielen, ist schon sehr alt.

Verbs

What is a verb?

Verbs describe the action (do, go etc.) or situation (be, have etc.) in a sentence or clause. They change in important ways depending on:

tense (past, present, future etc.)

person (I, you, it etc.)

number (singular, plural).

Most German verbs are 'weak' (regular), but some common ones are 'strong' (irregular) or 'mixed'. The part given in a dictionary is the **infinitive** – this almost always ends in –*en* and means '**to do**', '**to go**' etc.

1 Highlight the verbs in these sentences. Watch out – some have more than one verb.

a Ich verbringe ziemlich viel Zeit im Internet.

b – Wann beginnt der Film?
– Die erste Vorstellung ist um 19 Uhr.

c Ich möchte zwei Karten für morgen Abend reservieren.

d Ich habe dieses Handy letzte Woche gekauft, aber es funktioniert nicht.

e Ich bin auf den Weihnachtsmarkt gegangen und habe meine Geschenke gekauft.

f Letztes Jahr haben wir viel gegessen und getrunken und getanzt.

g Ich werde nächstes Jahr zum Musikfest in Nürnberg fahren.

Formal and informal usage

There are several words in German for 'you' and 'your'. It is important to choose the right one, depending whether you are being **formal or informal**.

2 Complete the explanation using the words in the box.

Young Germans speak and _____ to each other using the informal (_____) forms:

du (_____ person)

ihr (more than one _____).

_____ members also usually call each other *du*.

The possessive pronouns for informal '_____' are *dein/deine/dein; euer/eure/euer.*

The r_____ forms are: *dich* (accusative), *dir* (_____); *euch* (both _____ and dative).

When speaking or writing to someone _____ or not well known to you or in a position of _____, use the _____ (polite) *Sie* form.

This is the _____ for one and for more than one person.

The _____ pronoun for formal 'your' is *Ihr* for both singular and plural.

The reflexive form for formal *Sie* is _____ *sich.*

accusative	always	authority	dative	familiar
family	formal	older	one	person
possessive	reflexive	same	write	your

3 Now fill in the table.

Pronouns	Informal (familiar)		Formal (polite)	
	Singular	**Plural**	**Singular**	**Plural**
Nominative (you)		ihr		
Accusative (you)	dich			Sie
Dative (you)			Ihnen	
Possessive adj. (your)		euer/ eure/euer		
Reflexive (yourself)			sich	

Questions

TIPP

Questions are formed by turning the subject and verb around and sometimes adding a question word as well. (See also page 29 for more about question words.) Remember that the subject can be a whole phrase and not just one word.

Du hast einen Job. – *Hast du einen Job?*
Meine liebe Oma fährt nach Amerika. – *Fährt meine liebe Oma nach Amerika?*
Sie sind angekommen. – *Wann sind Sie angekommen?*

1 Make these statements into questions using the prompt where appropriate.

a Du gehst am Wochenende zur Party. (?)

_____ .

b Sie haben diesen Film gesehen. (*when?*)

_____ .

c Du bist zur Schule gekommen. (*how?*)

_____ .

d Frau Müller bleibt heute zu Hause. (?)

_____ .

e Er hat sich nicht gewaschen. (*why?*)

_____ .

f Die Kinder haben ihren Ball verloren. (*where?*)

_____ .

Negative

TIPP

To make a verb **negative**, add *nicht*. This usually goes at the end of a clause or sentence, but it must come before an adjective, a past participle or an infinitive.

Nicht can also be placed before a particular word or phrase to give it emphasis.

Dieses Buch gehört mir nicht.
This book doesn't belong to me.

Dieses Buch gehört nicht mir, sondern meinem Bruder.
This book doesn't belong to **me** but to my brother.

---

2 Are these sentences positive (P) or negative (N)?

a Das Spiel beginnt heute um neun. _____

b Ich habe meine Tennisschläger nicht. _____

c Es geht meiner Schwester nicht gut. _____

d Sie darf am Wochenende nicht mitkommen. _____

e Wir fahren nach dem Frühstück los. _____

f Ich kann das nicht kaufen, weil ich kein Geld habe. _____

TIPP

Remember that *kein* + noun means 'not a ...'. This is slightly different from English. For example, if you want to say 'I <u>don't have</u> a pen', you need to think of it as 'I have <u>no pen</u>' – *Ich habe keinen Kuli.* (See also page 11.)

3 Make these sentences negative by inserting *nicht* or using *kein* as appropriate.

a Ich kenne diesen Jungen.

_____ .

b Wir haben dieses Buch gelesen.

_____ .

c Meine Mutter hat einen Wagen.

_____ .

d Also kann ich mit ihr fahren.

_____ .

e Unsere Sporthalle ist sehr modern.

_____ .

f Ich esse dein Stück Kuchen.

_____ .

g Wir möchten eine Party zum Geburtstag haben.

_____ .

h Ich darf die Ohrringe kaufen, weil ich viel Geld habe.

_____ .

Modal verbs

TIPP

Six irregular verbs are known as **modal verbs**:

dürfen	to be allowed to
können	to be able to, 'can'
mögen	to like to
müssen	to have to, 'must'
sollen	to be supposed to, 'ought'
wollen	to want to

They normally need another verb to complete their meaning – this verb is in the infinitive and goes to the end of the clause. (See page 66 for more practice of word order.)

*Ich **kann** morgen nicht **arbeiten**.*
I cannot work tomorrow.

1 Underline the modal verbs and circle the infinitives in these sentences (if there is one). Then translate each sentence into English.

a Wir wollen am Wochenende Handball spielen.

_____ .

b Wann kannst du mir ein Computerspiel kaufen?

_____ ?

c Ich darf im Sommer nach Spanien fahren.

_____ .

d Heute soll ich lernen, aber ich will nicht.

_____ .

e Meine Eltern mögen es nicht, wenn ich spät nach Hause komme.

_____ .

f Ich mag nicht tanzen, weil ich nicht gut tanzen kann.

_____ .

g Wann musst du nach Hause gehen?

_____ ?

h Können Sie diese Flaschen bitte zum Recycling bringen?

_____ ?

TIPP

Sometimes modal verbs do not need an infinitive because the meaning is clear enough without one. Often, the missing verb is 'do': *Das kann ich nicht.* I can't (do that). Or 'go': *Ich will nach Hause.* I want to go home.

2 Match the pairs.

1 Wir wollen ein Eis.		**a**	He's good at German.
2 Ich muss mal!		**b**	I don't like (doing) that.
3 Er kann gut Deutsch.		**c**	We want an ice cream.
4 Sie muss jetzt zur Schule.		**d**	What are you allowed to do at school?
5 Das mag ich nicht.		**e**	She has to go to school now.
6 Was dürft ihr in der Schule?		**f**	I need the toilet!

TIPP

Notice the difference between *ich muss nicht* and *ich darf nicht*:

Ich muss nicht früh ins Bett gehen.
I don't have to go to bed early (but it would be better if I did).

Ich darf nicht früh ins Bett gehen.
I must not go to bed early (I'm not allowed to).

3 Write in German two things that you don't have to do, and two that you're not allowed to do. Give the English translation.

a Ich muss nicht _____

_____ .

b Ich muss nicht _____

_____ .

c Ich muss nicht _____

_____ .

d Ich muss nicht _____

_____ .

In the present tense, modal verbs are only slightly irregular in the singular. Most of them have a vowel change in the singular, but the *ich* and *er/sie/es* forms are the same, which makes things easier.

Impersonal verbs

Some common verbs are known as **impersonal verbs**. They are only used in the *es* form in certain phrases, and sometimes even the word *es* is missed out.

4 Complete the table of the present tense of all six modals.

	dürfen	können	mögen
Meaning	to be allowed to		to like
ich	darf		
du		kannst	
er/sie/es			mag
wir			
ihr	dürft		
Sie			
sie		können	

	müssen	söllen	wollen
Meaning		to be supposed to	
ich		soll	
du	musst		
er/sie/es			will
wir	müssen		
ihr		sollt	
Sie			wollen
sie			

1 Match the pairs.

1 Es gibt keine Marmelade.
2 Es gibt nur drei Eier.
3 Es tut mir Leid.
4 Wie geht's?
5 Es geht mir gut.
6 Es geht mir nicht gut.
7 Mir ist kalt.
8 Mir ist heiß.
9 Mir ist sehr schlecht.
10 Schmeckt dir das Essen?
11 Danke. Es schmeckt mir.
12 Es gefällt mir, wenn du lächelst.

a I am not well.
b I am sorry.
c I feel very sick.
d Thanks. I like it.
e There is no jam.
f Do you like the meal?
g I like it when you smile.
h I am well.
i There are only three eggs.
j I feel hot.
k How are you?
l I feel cold.

5 Translate these sentences into German. Remember to put the infinitive (if there is one) at the end.

a I'm supposed to go into town today. _____

b I'm not allowed to go to the cinema. _____

c They want to watch television. _____

d Can you (*du*) speak French? _____

e The teachers have to work every evening. _____

(See page 79 for more help with modal verbs.)

Separable and inseparable verbs

In German, as in English, many verbs come in two parts. If the verb is **separable**, the two parts do not usually come next to one another in a sentence. If the verb is **inseparable**, they do.

The verb *fernsehen*, for example, is **separable**. The *sehen* part follows the usual rules for verbs, and the separable prefix *fern* goes to the end of the sentence: *Ich **sehe** jeden Abend eine Stunde **fern**. −* I watch television for an hour every night.

The verb *bekommen* is **inseparable**. The prefix stays attached to the verb: *Ich **be**komme eine Medaille. −* I get a medal.

Here are some **separable verbs** you might use. In the infinitive, they are always joined together.

abfahren	to set off	*sich ausruhen*	to have a rest
abholen	to meet (= pick up, fetch)	*aussteigen*	to get off (bus)
abschließen	to lock (up)	*sich ausziehen*	to get undressed
abspülen	to wash up	*einkaufen*	to shop, go shopping
abtrocknen	to dry up	*einschlafen*	to go to sleep
anhalten	to stop (vehicles)	*einsteigen*	to get on (bus)
ankommen	to arrive	*fernsehen*	to watch TV
annehmen	to accept	*sich hinlegen*	to lie down
anrufen	to call (= telephone), phone	*sich hinsetzen*	to sit down
anschauen	to look at	*mitkommen*	to come with
sich ansehen	to watch	*mitnehmen*	to take (with you)
anspringen	to start (cars)	*umsteigen*	to change (e.g. trains)
sich anziehen	to get dressed	*sich umziehen*	to get changed
auffüllen	to fill up (cup)	*vorbeifahren an*	to go past (by car)
aufhören	to stop (doing something)	*vorbeigehen an*	to go past (on foot)
aufpassen	to pay attention	*vorbereiten*	to prepare
aufräumen	to tidy up, clear away	*vorziehen*	to prefer
aufstehen	to get up, to stand up	*weggehen*	to go away
aufwachen	to wake up	*wegwerfen*	to throw away
ausgeben	to spend (money)	*weitermachen*	to continue (e.g. studies)
ausgehen	to go out	*zuhören*	to listen to
auskommen mit	to get on with	*zunehmen*	to grow (= get bigger)
auspacken	to unpack	*zurückkommen*	to return, come/go back

1 In the list above, highlight the prefix of each verb (e.g. **ab**holen). Now look at the part after the prefix. In another colour, highlight the ones that you already know (e.g. an**kommen**). Tick the full separable verbs that you already know or can easily work out. Learn as many of the others as possible.

2 Highlight both parts of the separable verbs in these sentences, then translate into English.

  a Der Zug kommt um 14 Uhr in Köln an.
  _____

  b Ich wache immer vor meiner Schwester auf.
  _____

  c Samstags kaufe ich mit meinen Freunden in der Stadt ein.
  _____

  d Mein Brieffreund packt seinen Koffer aus.
  _____

  e Am Sonntag bereitet mein Vater das Mittagessen vor.
  _____

These prefixes are inseparable and can never be split from the rest of the verb: *be-, emp-, ent-, er-, ge-, miss-, ver-, zer-*.
Here are some **inseparable verbs** you might use.

beginnen	to begin/start	*übernachten*	to stay the night
begrüßen	to greet, welcome	*unterschreiben*	to sign
bekommen	to receive, get	*verbieten*	to forbid
benutzen	to use	*verbringen*	to spend (time)
beschreiben	to describe	*verdienen*	to earn
besprechen	to discuss	*vergessen*	to forget
bestellen	to order (e.g. in restaurant)	*verkaufen*	to sell
besuchen	to visit	*verlassen*	to leave (place)
bezahlen	to pay (for)	*verlieren*	to lose
empfehlen	to recommend	*vermieten*	to rent/hire out
enthalten	to contain	*verpassen*	to miss (bus)
sich entscheiden	to decide	*verstehen*	to understand
erreichen	to reach	*versuchen*	to try (to do something)
erzählen	to tell	*wiederholen*	to repeat
gewinnen	to win	*zerstören*	to destroy

3 In the list above, highlight in one colour the inseparable prefix of each verb (e.g. beginnen). Now look at the part of the verb after the prefix. In another colour, highlight the ones that you already know (e.g. bekommen).
Put a tick next to the full verbs that you already know. Try to learn as many of the others as possible.

4 Read the sentences and say whether the verbs are separable (S) or inseparable (I).

a Nach dem Mittagessen schlafen wir immer ein. _____

b Der Umweltschmutz zerstört unseren Planet. _____

c Ich versuche, etwas für unsere Umwelt zu tun. _____

d Wann stehst du am Wochenende normalerweise auf? _____

e Verstehst du die Frage nicht? _____

f Wir gewinnen nie im Lotto. _____

g Nach dem Essen spüle ich manchmal ab, aber nicht oft! _____

h Füllst du bitte meine Tasse auf? _____

5 Translate into German.

a We usually get up at quarter to seven.

_____.

b My mother prepares breakfast for us.

_____.

c I leave the house at half past seven.

_____.

d The bus arrives quite quickly at school.

_____.

e I discuss my homework with my friends.

_____.

f We get on well with the teachers.

_____.

See page 50 for practice using separable and inseparable verbs in the perfect tense.

Reflexive verbs

TIPP

Reflexive verbs need a pronoun to complete their meaning. Most take the accusative reflexive pronoun, but a few use the dative form (see Pronouns, page 34).

*Ich interessiere **mich** für Sport.* – I'm interested in sport.

*Ich mache **mir** Sorgen um Jochen.* – I'm worried about Jochen.

1 Complete the table.

Subject (nominative)	Reflexive pronouns	
	Accusative	**Dative**
		mir
du	dich	
er, sie, es		sich
	uns	
ihr		euch
Sie	sich	
sie		sich

2 Fill the gaps in the meanings of some common accusative reflexive verbs:

sich anziehen	to get dressed
sich ausziehen	to get _____
sich umziehen	to get changed
sich ausruhen	to have a rest
sich beeilen	to hurry
sich duschen	to have a _____
sich erinnern (an etwas)	to remember (something)
sich freuen (auf etwas)	to look _____ (to something)
sich fühlen	to feel
sich hinlegen	to lie down
sich hinsetzen	to sit _____
sich interessieren (für etwas)	to be _____ (in something)
sich sonnen	to _____

3 Draw lines to match the sentence halves.

1 Wann ziehst du
2 Vor dem Spiel ziehe ich
3 So spät schon?! Ich muss
4 Meine Eltern freuen
5 Morgens werden wir
6 Erinnert ihr
7 Fühlen Sie
8 Vielleicht sollten Sie
9 Wofür interessiert sich

a euch an Ahmed?
b mich wirklich beeilen.
c sich ein bisschen hinsetzen.
d dich normalerweise an?
e sich nicht so gut?
f deine Brieffreundin?
g uns am Strand sonnen.
h mich natürlich um.
i sich auf die Ferien.

4 Choose five verbs from the list in Exercise 2 and for each verb write a sentence about yourself or a friend. Use the examples in Exercise 3 to help you:

e.g. (sich interessieren) *Ich interessiere mich sehr für Sport.*

a _____

_____

_____

b _____

_____

_____

c _____

_____

_____

d _____

_____

_____

e _____

_____

_____

Verbs that take the **dative reflexive** pronoun often have a direct object in the sentence. Compare these sentences:

Ich ziehe mich vor dem Frühstück an. – I get dressed before breakfast.

(*mich* = accusative reflexive pronoun – I dress 'myself')

Ich ziehe mir einen Pullover an. –I put a jumper on.

(*einen Pullover* = accusative direct object, the thing I'm putting on)

(*mir* = dative reflexive pronoun to show that I'm putting the jumper onto myself and not anybody else)

Here are some common **dative reflexive verbs**:

sich (etwas) ansehen	to watch (something)
sich (etwas) anziehen	to put (something) on
sich (etwas) ausziehen	to take (something) off
sich (die Haare) bürsten	to brush (your hair)
sich (die Haare) kämmen	to comb (your hair)
sich (etwas) kaufen	to buy oneself (something)
sich (etwas) leisten	to afford/treat oneself (to something)
sich Sorgen machen	to be worried
sich (etwas) überlegen	to think about, consider (something)
sich vorstellen	to imagine
sich (die Hände) waschen	to wash (your hands)
sich (etwas) wünschen	to wish (for something)

5 Highlight the verbs you already know in this list. Write down some ways to help you remember the ones you don't yet know.

_____

_____

_____

_____

_____

6 For each sentence write D if it contains a dative reflexive pronoun, and write A if it has an accusative reflexive. For many of the pronouns you cannot tell whether they are accusative or dative so you will have to use other clues.

a Mach dir keine Sorgen um deinen Freund – alles wird gut gehen. _____

b Ich habe mir eben das Gesicht gewaschen. _____

c Abends ziehe ich mich vor dem Essen um. _____

d Sie können sich kein neues Auto leisten. _____

e Er zieht sich eine Jacke an, weil es kalt ist. _____

f Wir interessieren uns nicht für Rockmusik. _____

g Die Spieler mussten sich nach dem Spiel duschen. _____

7 Translate into German.

a I wash my hands before lunch.

_____

_____ .

b He's buying himself a new computer.

_____

_____ .

c We can afford a cake.

_____

_____ .

d Have you (*du*) cleaned your teeth?

_____

_____ ?

e She's putting a jumper on.

_____

_____ .

f I'm worried about my friend.

_____

_____ .

Tenses

Present tense

TIPP

The **present tense** is used as in English, but, unlike in English, there is only one form of the present in German. Look at these examples:

Ich spiele jeden Samstag Fußball. − <u>I play</u> football every Saturday.

Was <u>spielst du</u> jetzt? − What <u>are you playing</u> now?

Ich spiele Fußball. − <u>I'm playing</u> football.

Du spielst nicht in der Mannschaft! − <u>You don't play</u> in the team!

Doch! <u>Ich spiele</u> doch in der Mannschaft. − Yes, <u>I **do** play</u> in the team.

1 Find the German for these sentences. Write the appropriate letter (a–f). You will use some letters more than once.

1 Do you listen to music?   _____
2 You fall asleep.   _____
3 We're listening to music.   _____
4 Are you falling asleep?   _____
5 We listen to music.   _____
6 You're not falling asleep.   _____
7 You're falling asleep.   _____
8 We don't listen to music.   _____
9 Are you listening to music?   _____
10 You do fall asleep.   _____

a Wir hören Musik.
b Wir hören keine Musik.
c Hörst du Musik?
d Du schläfst ein.
e Schläfst du ein?
f Du schläfst nicht ein.

TIPP

Most verbs have the same **endings** in the **present tense**.

Weak (regular) verbs

TIPP

Weak (regular) verbs form the present tense by taking *-en* from the infinitive (to give the **stem**) and adding these endings:

ich	**-e**	wir	**-en**
du	**-st**	ihr	**-t**
er/sie/es/ man	**-t**	Sie	**-en**
		sie	**-en**

If the stem ends in *-t* or *-d* or three consonants (e.g. *-chn*, *-ckn*), add an extra *-e* before the *du, er/sie/es/man* and *ihr* endings. This is just to make pronunciation easier.

infinitive	arbeit**en**	bad**en**	zeichn**en**	trockn**en**
stem	arbeit–	bad–	zei**chn**–	tro**ckn**–
er/sie/es	arbei**tet**	bad**et**	zeichn**et**	trockn**et**

2 Put these infinitives into the correct present tense forms. Look out for one separable and one reflexive verb!

a wohnen   ich   _____
b arbeiten   du   _____
c stellen   er   _____
d sich bürsten sie   _____
e brauchen   es   _____
f machen   man   _____
g hassen   wir   _____
h mieten   ihr   _____
i einkaufen   Sie   _____
j sagen   sie   _____

Strong (irregular) verbs

3 Choose the correct verb in the box to complete these sentences.

Marina (1) _____ jeden Abend ein paar Stunden fern. In ihrem

Zimmer (2) _____ es einen großen Fernseher. Sie (3) _____,

dass zu viel Fernsehen nicht gut ist, aber das (4) _____ nicht.

Manchmal (5) _____ sie vor dem Fernseher ein.

Ihre Schwester Linda ist sportlich. Sie (6) _____ oft im Park und

(7) _____ sich mit Freunden im Sportzentrum. Die Eltern sagen:

„Warum (8) _____ ihr nicht zusammen zum Sportzentrum?" Linda

(9) _____ also ihre Schwester mit. Jetzt (10) _____ Marina

ihr Zimmer viel öfter. Sie (11) _____ zweimal in der Woche mit ihrer

Schwester zum Fitness-Klub. „(12) _____ ihr! Das ist viel besser",

sagen die Eltern.

| fahrt fährt gibt hilft läuft nimmt |
| schläft seht sieht trifft verlässt weiß |

TIPP

Strong (irregular) verbs in the **present tense** almost all have the same endings as weak verbs (–e, –st, –t, –en, –t, –en, –en). There may be a change to the **stem**, but **only** in the *du* and *er/sie/es* forms, and the stem change will be the same for both forms.

Some of these changes follow a pattern, but if you're not sure, check in the table of strong and irregular verbs (pages 71–72). The most common stem changes are:

e– i or ie (e.g. g**e**ben – du g**i**bst, er/sie/es g**i**bt; s**e**hen – du s**ie**hst, er/sie/es s**ie**ht)

a– ä (e.g. f**a**hren – du f**ä**hrst, er/sie/es f**ä**hrt; l**au**fen – du l**äu**fst, er l**äu**ft)

4 Complete the table with the correct present tense forms. Look out for one separable and one reflexive verb!

	Infinitive	ich	du	er/sie/es	ihr	Sie
1	sprechen					
2	helfen					
3	essen					
4	halten					
5	lassen					
6	nehmen					
7	fahren					
8	sich waschen					
9	fallen					
10	einschlafen					

5 Complete the sentences with the correct form of the verbs. Then translate into English – think carefully about how you translate the present tense.

a Normalerweise (nehmen) _____ Wolfgang den

Bus, aber heute (fahren) _____ er mit dem Rad

zur Schule.

_____

_____.

b (essen) _____ ihr jeden Tag etwas in der Pause?

_____?

c Ich (waschen) _____ mir immer das Gesicht
nach dem Essen.

_____.

d Warum (laufen) _____ du weg? Es (geben)

_____ noch viel zu sehen.

_____

_____.

The irregular verbs *haben*, *sein* and *werden* are widely used and need to be learnt. See also pages 48–52, 56 and 80.

6 Complete the explanation using words from the box.

The verb *haben* means 'to have'. It is only slightly

(1) _____ in the present tense – no letter -*b*- in

the (2) _____ and *er/sie/es* forms.

In the (3) _____ tense, most verbs use *haben*

as the (4) _____ (*ich* **habe** ... *gespielt* etc.). In

English, 'to be' is used to express hunger and thirst, but

in German you have to use (5) _____ and say 'I

have hunger/thirst' etc. (*ich* **habe** *Hunger; ihr*

(6) _____ *Durst*).

| auxiliary | *du* | haben | habt | irregular | perfect |

7 Complete the table. The shaded areas show where the verb is irregular.

	haben	*to have*
ich		
du	hast	
er/sie/es		*he/she/it has*
wir	haben	
ihr	habt	
Sie		
sie	haben	*they have*

8 Complete the explanation using words from the box.

The verb *sein* means '(1) _____.' It is very

(2) _____ in all forms but it is widely used.

Many verbs use *sein* as the auxiliary to form the perfect

(3) _____, (*er* (4) _____ ... *gegangen*

etc.), but this is still translated as 'I (5) _____

gone' etc.

| have | irregular | *ist* | tense | to be |

9 Complete the table.

	sein	*to be*
ich		*I am*
du	bist	
er/sie/es		
wir	sind	
ihr	seid	
Sie	sind	*you are*
sie		

10 Complete the explanation using words from the box.

The verb *werden* means '(1) _____' or 'to be

going to be' and is often used to talk about

(2) _____ and careers (*er wird Lehrer*).

Like most irregular verbs in the present tense it only

changes in the (3) _____ and *er/sie/es* forms.

One of its main uses is with the infinitive of another

verb to form the (4) _____ tense (*ich werde ...*

arbeiten etc.). In that case it means 'I will work' or 'I

(5) _____ to work' etc.

| am going | *du* | future | jobs | to become |

11 Complete the table.

	werden	*to become (etc.)*
ich		
du	wirst	*you become*
er/sie/es	wird	
wir	werden	
ihr		
Sie	werden	
sie		

12 Add the correct part of *haben*, *sein* or *werden*.

a _____ du Hunger?

b Wann _____ die Sommerferien?

c Was _____ du nächstes Jahr machen?

d Wie viel Geld _____ er?

e Ich sehe euch nicht. Wo _____ ihr?

f Wann _____ deine ältere Schwester Ärztin?

Perfect tense

1 Find the German for these sentences. Write the appropriate number (1–6). You will use each number more than once.

a I have played table tennis. _____

b Haven't you been playing table tennis? _____

c He's gone to Berlin. _____

d Did you play table tennis? _____

e He didn't go to Berlin. _____

f Has he gone to Berlin? _____

g Have you played table tennis? _____

h I played table tennis. _____

i He hasn't gone to Berlin. _____

j Didn't you play table tennis? _____

k Have you been playing table tennis? _____

l Did he go to Berlin? _____

m He went to Berlin. _____

n Haven't you played table tennis? _____

o I've been playing table tennis. _____

1 Ich habe Tischtennis gespielt.

2 Hast du Tischtennis gespielt?

3 Habt ihr keinen Tischtennis gespielt?

4 Er ist nach Berlin gefahren.

5 Ist er nach Berlin gefahren?

6 Er ist nicht nach Berlin gefahren.

2 Underline the auxiliary and circle the past participle in each sentence. Translate each sentence into English.

a Was hast du gestern gemacht?

_____.

b Ich bin mit Max in die Stadt gefahren.

_____.

c Wir haben neue Kleidung gekauft.

_____.

d Nach dem Abendessen habe ich Karten gespielt.

_____.

e Wann bist du ins Bett gegangen?

_____.

f Gegen 11 Uhr ist meine Mutter ins Zimmer gekommen.

_____.

g Sie hat „Gute Nacht" gesagt.

_____.

h Aber dann habe ich das Buch gelesen, das du mir gegeben hast.

_____.

i Dieses Buch habe habe ich sehr interessant gefunden.

_____.

j Heute Morgen habe ich lange geschlafen.

_____.

3 Write the past participle of these verbs.

a tanzen   ich habe _____

b sparen   du hast _____

c reichen   er hat _____

d machen   sie hat _____

e arbeiten   es hat _____

f mieten   wir haben _____

g lernen   ihr habt _____

h hören   Sie haben _____

i leben   sie haben _____

4 Choose five verbs from Exercise 3 and write a sentence in the perfect tense for each.

a _____ .

b _____ .

c _____ .

d _____ .

e _____ .

5 Write the appropriate perfect tense next to the infinitive. Choose from the box.

a nehmen   _____

b helfen   _____

c bleiben   _____

d essen   _____

e beginnen   _____

f halten   _____

g brechen   _____

h sein   _____

i fahren   _____

j schließen   _____

k gehen   _____

l schreiben   _____

m stehen   _____

n treffen   _____

o werden   _____

p sprechen   _____

> hast ... gehalten
> hat ... **gegessen**
> sind ... gefahren
> habt ... getroffen
> habe ... geholfen
> bin ... gegangen
> haben ... gesprochen
> hat ... genommen
> seid ... gewesen
> hat ... gestanden
> ist ... geblieben
> haben ... gebrochen
> hat ... begonnen
> hast ... geschrieben
> haben ... geschlossen
> ist ... geworden

6 Write the infinitive of these perfect tense verbs and the meaning.

		infinitive	meaning
a	hat ... gebracht	_____	_____
b	hat ... gedacht	_____	_____
c	hat ... gehabt	_____	_____
d	hat ... gekannt	_____	_____
e	hat ... gesandt	_____	_____
f	hat ... gewusst	_____	_____

> senden   bringen   wissen
> kennen   haben   denken

7 Complete each sentence with the verb in brackets. The prefix is in bold and there is an indication of whether the verb is weak (**W**), strong (**S**) or mixed (**M**).

a Am Wochenende habe ich mein Zimmer _____. (**auf**räumen) (W)

b Wir haben gestern Abend bei Freunden _____. (**fern**sehen) (S)

c Du bist sehr spät _____. (**ein**schlafen) (S)

d Ich bin heute um 6 Uhr _____. (**auf**wachen) (W)

e Ich habe mich sehr warm _____. (**an**ziehen) (S)

f Hast du dieses Formular schon _____? (**aus**füllen) (W)

g Oliver ist zum Jugendklub _____. (**mit**kommen) (S)

h Er hat seine Gitarre _____. (**mit**bringen) (M)

8 Choose a past participle to complete each sentence.

a Erik hat 50 Euro von seiner Oma _____.

b Wir haben das Thema „Jugend und Politik" _____.

c Die chinesischen Besucher haben kein Wort _____.

d Wir haben unsere Gäste offiziell im Rathaus _____.

e Ich habe die Gruppe mit meinem neuen Apparat _____.

f Hast du von der Telefonzelle oder vom Handy _____?

g Ich habe _____, mein neues Handy zu benutzen.

h Habt ihr diese Bonbons _____? Sie schmecken toll!

> begrüßt   diskutiert   erhalten   fotografiert
> probiert   telefoniert   verstanden   versucht

9 Which auxiliary is used in the following sentences? Write *haben* or *sein*. Then write the infinitive of the verb used.

	Aux.	**Infinitive**
a Wann bist du nach Hause gegangen?	_____	_____
b Wir haben die letzte Stunde frei gehabt.	_____	_____
c In unserer Stadt ist Recycling viel besser geworden.	_____	_____
d Habt ihr den Film im Ersten gesehen?	_____	_____
e Zum Geburtstag habe ich neue Socken bekommen!	_____	_____
f In den Ferien sind wir zu Hause geblieben.	_____	_____
g Wann seid ihr nach der Party aufgestanden?	_____	_____
h Bastian hat mich zum Konzert eingeladen.	_____	_____

10 Fill the gap with the correct form of *haben* or *sein*.

a Wir _____ im August nach Amerika geflogen.

b Mein Onkel _____ einen Hubschrauber geflogen.

c Ich _____ mein neues Pony zum ersten Mal geritten.

d _____ ihr am Strand geritten?

e Nach der Schule _____ sie sich umgezogen.

f Meine beste Freundin _____ nach München umgezogen.

habe	haben	hat	ist	Seid	sind

11 Write full sentences in German following the prompts:

e.g. ich – sich duschen   vor dem Frühstück
Ich habe mich vor dem Frühstück geduscht.

a ihr – sich sonnen – jeden Tag – in Spanien

_____

_____.

b wir – sich anziehen – für das Konzert

_____

_____.

c du – sich interessieren – als Kind – für Plüschtiere ?

_____

_____.

d ich – sich kaufen – heute – ein neues Hemd

_____

_____.

e nach dem Spiel – sie (*they*) – sich hinsetzen

_____

_____.

12 Complete the summary of the perfect tense.

The perfect tense is used to talk about the

(1) _____. It is made up of two parts – the

(2) _____ and the (3) _____.

For most verbs, the auxiliary is (4) _____. This

applies to all (5) _____ verbs. Some verbs use

(6) _____ as the auxiliary. These verbs often

involve a change of (7) _____ or state.

Weak verbs form the past participle with the prefix

(8) _____ and the ending (9) _____.

Most strong verbs form the past participle with *ge-* and

the ending (10) _____. There is often a change

to the (11) _____.

(12) _____ and mixed verbs have the weak

prefix and ending, but the stem usually changes.

Separable verbs put *-ge-* in the (13) _____ of

the past participle (e.g. *fern**ge**sehen*).

Inseparable and *-ieren* verbs (14) _____ put

ge- on the past participle.

> auxiliary   do not   *-en*   ge-   haben   middle
> Modal   past   past participle   place
> reflexive   sein   stem   -t

13 Write the perfect tense of these verbs.

a sich waschen	ich	_____
b sagen	du	_____
c müssen	er	_____
d ankommen	sie (*she*)	_____
e sein	es	_____
f finden	wir	_____
g lieben	ihr	_____
h schwimmen	Sie	_____
i sich befinden	du	_____
j verwenden	ich	_____

14 Rewrite these sentences in the perfect tense.

a Wir machen Interviews in der Klasse.

_____

b Es tut mir Leid!

_____

c Ich fliege nach Paris.

_____

d Du kriegst gute Noten.

_____

e Herbert fängt in der Schule später als ich an.

_____

f Elke isst manchmal im Café.

_____

g Die Deutschstunde ist zu kurz.

_____

h Ich wähle Fremdsprachen.

_____

i Du überlegst dir deine Wahlfächer.

_____

j Sie wird Ingenieurin.

_____

15 Choose eight different verbs and for each write a sentence about what you did last week.

a _____.

b _____.

c _____.

d _____.

e _____.

f _____.

g _____.

h _____.

Imperfect tense (simple past)

In German, one of the easiest ways to talk about the past is by using the **imperfect tense** (also known as the **simple past**). It is generally more common in written than in spoken language.

ich spielte – I played; *er war* – he was; *sie hatten* – they had; *wir mussten* – we had to.

To form the **imperfect tense, weak verbs** add these endings to the stem:

ich	-te
du	-test
er/sie/es	-te
wir	-ten
ihr	-tet
Sie	-ten
sie	-ten

Note that these are mostly similar to the present tense endings with –*t*- inserted.

Sometimes an extra –*e*- is added to help pronunciation (*sie wart**eten***).

1 Write the appropriate form of the imperfect tense.

a telefonieren   er   _____

b sagen   sie (*she*)   _____

c macht   es   _____

d einkaufen   ich   _____

e antworten   du   _____

f lernen   man   _____

g sich setzen   ihr   _____

h studieren   Sie   _____

i sparen   wir   _____

j kriegen   sie (*they*)   _____

In the **imperfect tense, mixed and modal verbs** have the same endings as weak verbs, but the stem may change: *bringen – ich brach**te**; haben – du hat**test**; müssen – er muss**te***.

2 Match these imperfect tenses (1–12) to their infinitives (a–l).

1	ich brachte	a	dürfen
2	sie dachte	b	können
3	er durfte	c	senden
4	es hatte	d	wollen
5	wir kannten	e	bringen
6	ich konnte	f	haben
7	ihr mochtet	g	mögen
8	du musstest	h	denken
9	Sie sandten	i	wissen
10	sie sollten	j	müssen
11	wir wussten	k	sollen
12	er wollte	l	kennen

3 Choose five verbs from Exercises 1 and 2. Write a sentence for each in the imperfect tense.

a _____.

b _____.

c _____.

d _____.

e _____.

4 First do Exercise 5 on page 54 and look at the table of stem changes. Write these verbs in the imperfect tense. Then complete each sentence in a way that makes sense!

a kommen

Er _____.

b bleiben

Ich _____.

c sich waschen

Wir _____.

d fliegen

Sie _____.

e beginnen

Es _____.

Strong verbs usually change the stem in the **imperfect** and they have a different set of endings:

ich	–		wir	–en
du	–st		ihr	–t
er/sie/ es/man	–		Sie	–en
			sie	–en

e.g. *fahren – ich fuhr; sehen – er sah; nehmen – wir nahmen*

5 Fill in the table to show the similarities and differences between weak, mixed and strong verbs in the imperfect tense.

Weak	Mixed	Strong
stem is regular	stem usually (1) _____	(2) _____ usually changes
most endings are similar to the (3) _____ tense endings, but with an extra -*t(e)*-	endings are the same as the (4) _____ verbs in the imperfect	endings are exactly the same as the present tense endings except for (5) _____ and *er/sie/es* forms
ich and *er/sie/es* forms are exactly the (6) _____	*ich* and (7) _____ forms are exactly the same	*ich* and *er/sie/es* forms are (8) _____ the same

Here is a table of some imperfect stem changes.

Main vowel in infinitive	Main vowel in imperfect	Strong verb examples (infinitive)	Mixed/modal verb examples (infinitive)
a	ie	braten, fallen, halten, lassen, schlafen	
a	u	fahren, schlagen, waschen	
e	a	brechen, essen, geben, helfen, nehmen, sehen, sprechen, stehen, sterben, treffen, werfen	denken, kennen, senden
i	a	beginnen, gewinnen, schwimmen, sitzen, springen, trinken	bringen
ei	ie	bleiben, heißen, leihen, scheinen, schreiben, schreien, steigen	
ie	o	bieten, fliegen, frieren, schließen, verlieren, wiegen, ziehen	
ei/e	i	reiten, schneiden, gehen	
au/u	ie	laufen, rufen	
u/o/ie	a	tun, kommen, liegen	
ü	u		dürfen, müssen
ö	o		können, mögen
e/i	u		werden, wissen
sein	war	(sein *is very irregular*)	

Pluperfect tense

The **pluperfect tense** describes what **had happened** before another event in the past. It is formed like the perfect tense, but using the imperfect tense of *haben* or *sein* + past participle, e.g. *wir hatten gespielt; sie war gegangen*.

	haben	**sein**	
ich	hatte	war	
du	hattest	warst	
er/sie/es/man	hatte	war	
wir	hatten	waren	*+ past participle*
ihr	hattet	wart	
Sie	hatten	waren	
sie	hatten	waren	

1 Underline the auxiliary and the past participle of the verbs that are in the pluperfect tense.

a Im Jahr 2000 arbeitete sie in Berlin, und vorher hatte sie an der Uni studiert.

b Er hatte seine Kreditkarte verloren und musste der Bank Bescheid sagen.

c Max hatte nicht gemerkt, dass der Bus schon angekommen war.

d Wir waren so schnell gefahren, dass wir eine Viertelstunde zu früh ankamen.

e Vor zwei Jahren habe ich die *Fantastischen Vier* gemocht, aber davor hatte ich meistens *Rammstein* gehört.

f Sie haben gewonnen, weil sie vor dem Spiel lange trainiert hatten.

g Früher war ich nie in ein Konzert gegangen, aber dann hat mir meine Schwester zwei Karten geschenkt.

h Der Urlaub war toll – das hatte ich nicht erwartet!

i Oliver wollte mich ins Kino einladen, aber ich hatte den Film schon gesehen.

j Sie hatten Durst, weil sie das Wasser nicht getrunken hatten.

2 Put these verbs into the pluperfect tense. a–e take *haben*, f–j take *sein*.

a trinken ich

_____

b spielen wir

_____

c sich waschen sie (*they*)

_____

d verlieren du

_____

e regnen es

_____

f gehen sie (*she*)

_____

g bleiben ich

_____

h einsteigen er

_____

i sein es

_____

j fallen Sie

_____

3 Complete the sentences in the pluperfect tense using words from the box.

a Petra _____ die Antwort schon _____.

b Meine Eltern _____ zehn Minuten zu spät in Hamburg _____.

c Bastian _____ am Montag nicht zur Schule _____.

d Die drei Kinder _____ den Kuchen heimlich _____.

e Was _____ du vor der Deutschstunde _____?

f Und warum _____ du auf den Tisch _____?

hatte	hatten	hattest	war	waren	warst
angekommen	gegangen	gegessen			
gemacht	gesagt	gestiegen			

Future tense

1 Complete the present tense of *werden*.

ich _____

du wirst

er/sie/es _____

wir werden

ihr _____

Sie werden

sie _____

2 Underline the future tense in each sentence. Then translate each sentence into English.

a Hoffentlich werde ich gute Noten bekommen.

_____.

b Wirst du nächstes Jahr mit mir Deutsch studieren?

_____.

c In den Sommerferien wird mein Freund ein Praktikum bei VW machen.

_____.

d Ihr werdet wie immer mit dem Wohnwagen nach Frankreich fahren.

_____.

e Wenn das Wetter so schlecht bleibt, werden wir nach Hause gehen müssen.

_____.

3 Use the future tense to say three things about your plans for next year.

a _____

_____.

b _____

_____.

c _____

_____.

4 Translate these sentences into German – first use the present tense, then use the future tense. Think about the word order!

a Next week I'm going to France.

_____

_____.

_____

_____.

b In the summer holidays we're staying in Scotland.

_____

_____

_____

_____.

c After the German lesson you'll have maths.

_____

_____.

_____

_____.

d She'll drink a glass of water after lunch.

_____

_____.

_____

_____.

e Next month they're doing a work experience placement.

_____

_____.

_____

_____.

The conditional

The conditional means 'would do', 'would buy' etc. It is formed using *würde* + infinitive:

*Ich **würde** kein großes Auto **kaufen**.* – I **would** not **buy** a big car.

ich	würde	wir	würden	
du	würdest	ihr	würdet	+
er/sie/ es/man	würde	Sie	würden	*infinitive*
		sie	würden	

Modal and auxiliary verbs usually use the imperfect subjunctive to express the conditional, especially in *wenn* (**if**) clauses. The endings of the imperfect subjunctive are the same as on *würde* (see above): *haben – ich hätte; sein – ich wäre; können – ich könnte; sollen – ich sollte; mögen – ich möchte*.

   *Wenn ich reich **wäre**, **würde** ich mir einen besseren Computer **kaufen**.*
   If I **were** rich, **I'd buy** myself a better computer.

1 Underline the conditional and translate the sentences into English.

   a Mein Großvater würde nie ins Ausland fahren.

   _____.

   b Wir würden den ganzen Abend am Computer verbringen.

   _____.

   c Ich würde nicht in einem Büro arbeiten.

   _____.

   d Zu viele Hausaufgaben würden Schüler müde machen.

   _____.

   e Ihr würdet keine Zeit für Hobbys haben.

   _____.

   f Würdest du im Winter nach Spanien fahren?

   _____.

   g Wer würde 1000 Euro für ein Kleid ausgeben?

   _____.

   h Nach einem Jahr würden Sie uns vergessen.

   _____.

2 Put these verbs into the conditional.

   a gewinnen   er _____

   b aufstehen   ihr _____

   c sich duschen   wir _____

   d kosten   es _____

   e telefonieren   du _____

3 Match the German to the English.

   1 Wenn ich viel Geld hätte, würde ich nicht arbeiten.
   2 Er würde nicht zur Party kommen, wenn Alexa nicht da wäre.
   3 Wenn ich gut tanzen könnte, würde ich zur Party gehen.
   4 Wenn sie wählen dürfte, würde sie zu Hause bleiben.
   5 Wenn das Wetter besser wäre, würden wir öfter ausgehen.

   a If the weather were better we'd go out more often.
   b If I could dance well, I'd go to the party.
   c If I had lots of money, I wouldn't work.
   d If she could choose, she'd stay at home.
   e He wouldn't come to the party if Alexa wasn't there.

Constructions with the infinitive

1 Complete these sentences following the prompts.

a Du _____ heute eine Arbeit _____.
(*you have to write*)

b Was _____ wir nächste Woche _____?
(*will we do*)

c Ich _____ mir einen neuen Computer
_____. (*I would buy*)

d _____ ihr uns nach der Schule _____?
(*can you phone*)

e Im Winter _____ sie in die Schweiz
_____. (*she would go*)

2 Complete these sentences following the prompts.

a Ich hoffe, nächstes Jahr Deutsch _____.
(*to study*)

b Hast du versucht, früher _____? (*to get up*)

c Sie hat beschlossen, ein Jahr im Ausland
_____. (*to spend*)

d Es hat plötzlich begonnen, sehr stark _____.
(*to rain*)

e Ich habe heute keine Lust, gebratenes Hähnchen
_____. (*to eat*)

3 Draw lines to match the sentence halves.

1 Elena wird fleißiger lernen,	**a** ohne zu bezahlen?
2 Haben sie den Laden verlassen,	**b** ist sie aus dem Zimmer gegangen.
3 Welchen Bus nimmst du,	**c** muss man viel üben.
4 Sie hat eine Kritik geschrieben,	**d** um bessere Noten zu bekommen.
5 Um sehr gut zu spielen,	**e** ohne das Buch zu lesen.
6 Ohne ein einziges Wort zu sagen,	**f** um in die Stadtmitte zu kommen?

4 Complete these sentences with *zu* where necessary.

a Er wollte viel Geld _____, um eine Weltreise
_____. (verdienen/machen)

b Du sollst das _____, ohne den Mund
_____. (sagen/bewegen)

c Sie darf zum Stadion _____, um ihre
Lieblingsmannschaft _____. (gehen/sehen)

d Wann hoffen Sie, Ihren Führerschein _____?
(machen)

e Ohne Deutsch _____, kann man nicht alles
_____. (sprechen/verstehen)

f Wir haben vergessen, einen Pullover _____.
(mitnehmen)

The imperative

The **imperative** is used to give orders or instructions. Because there are three words for 'you' in German, there are three ways of forming the imperative:

- *du* form – take the *-st* off the *du* form of the verb and drop the *du*:

  du bleibst – **bleib!**

- *ihr* form – simply drop the *ihr*:

  ihr bleibt – **bleibt!**

- *Sie* form – simply invert the verb and the pronoun *Sie*:

  Sie bleiben – **bleiben Sie!**

The verb *sein* (to be) is irregular: *sei! seid! seien Sie!*

Reflexives need the appropriate pronoun (*dich/euch/sich*).

Separable verbs send the separable prefix to the end.

1 Your German penfriend's family are giving you instructions and telling you to do things. Put the infinitives into the appropriate imperative form:

e.g. sich hinsetzen   *Setz dich hin!*

a hereinkommen   _____

b mal nach Hause telefonieren   _____

c mehr essen   _____

d Deutsch sprechen   _____

e sich die Hände waschen   _____

f gut schlafen   _____

2 Your teacher is telling the class to do things. Rewrite these sentences in the imperative:

e.g. Könntet ihr nicht gut zuhören? *Hört gut zu!*

a Ihr müsst eine Arbeit schreiben!

_____!

b Ihr sollt Vokabeln lernen!

_____!

c Könntet ihr bitte schneller arbeiten?

_____!

d Ihr müsst rechtzeitig eure Hausaufgaben machen!

_____!

e Ihr sollt ruhig sein!

_____!

f Ihr dürft gut aufpassen!

_____!

3 Tell your friend's parents what to do in Berlin:

e.g. die Mauer besichtigen *Besichtigen Sie die Mauer!*

a die Museen besuchen

_____!

b in den großen Geschäften einkaufen

_____!

c die U-Bahn und Busse benutzen

_____!

d die Tiere im Zoo füttern

_____!

e sich eine Show ansehen

_____!

f im Café Kranzler Kaffee trinken

_____!

4 Change the following statements into the imperative.

a Ihr seht nicht zu viel fern. _____

_____!

b Du stehst früh auf. _____

_____!

c Sie sind um 10 Uhr da. _____

_____!

d Sie haben keine Angst. _____

_____!

e Du öffnest das Fenster. _____

_____!

f Ihr putzt euch die Nase. _____

_____!

Summary of verb type usage

1 Underline the verb in each sentence and say what tense it is. Remember, some verbs have two parts.

a Jürgen steht normalerweise ziemlich früh auf. _____

b Letzten Dienstag hat er den Bus verpasst. _____

c Er hatte seinen Wecker einfach nicht gehört. _____

d Er ist zur Bushaltestelle gerannt. _____

e Vielleicht würde er den Bus noch erreichen. _____

f Der Bus war aber schon abgefahren. _____

g Er musste auf den nächsten Bus warten. _____

h Am Wochenende wird er sich einen besseren Wecker kaufen! _____

2 Put these verbs into the present tense.

a samstags spät aufstehen

Ich _____.

b ein Bad nehmen

Sie (*she*) _____.

c mit einem Freund telefonieren

Du _____.

d sich mit ihr treffen

Er _____.

e sich ein Eis kaufen

Ihr _____.

f nach Hause fahren

Du _____.

g ein bisschen fernsehen

Wir _____.

3 Complete the sentences using the perfect (**P**) and imperfect (**I**) tenses to talk about a past holiday.

a nach Griechenland fahren (**P**)

Ich _____.

b in einem Hotel wohnen (**P**)

Wir _____.

c gut sein (**I**)

Das Essen _____.

d viele Ruinen besichtigen ? (**P**)

_____ ihr _____?

e sich am Strand sonnen können (**I**)

Man _____.

f leider arbeiten müssen (**I**)

Wir _____.

g morgens um 4 Uhr ankommen (**P**)

Er _____.

4 Say what will or would happen.

a Ich _____ viel Geld gewinnen. (*will*)

b Das _____ toll sein! (*would*)

c Wir _____ uns neue Kleidung _____. (*will buy*)

d Sie _____ lange auf Partys _____. (*would stay*)

e Wann _____ ihr _____? (*would get up*)

f Was _____ Sie als Beruf _____? (*will do*)

g Ich _____ freiwillig _____. (*would work*)

Word order

Main clauses

TIPP

> The **main verb** is always the **second idea** (but not necessarily the second word) in a German sentence. If there are two verbs that belong together (e.g. *ich muss ... lachen*) the main verb is the one that changes with the subject (i.e. *ich muss*). Similarly, in the perfect tense, the verb affected by the 'verb second' rule is the auxiliary (e.g. *ich habe ... gelacht*).

1 Highlight the main verb in these sentences.

  a Basel liegt im Norden der Schweiz.

  b Drei Städte in der Schweiz, Deutschland und Frankreich teilen sich den Flughafen.

  c Viele weltberühmte Pharma-Industrien haben ihren Sitz in der Stadt.

  d Die Altstadt hat schöne alte Gebäude.

  e Es gibt viele Besucher im Februar wegen Fasnacht.

  f Alt und Jung feiern bis spät in die Nacht.

  g Man kann jeden Tag große Schiffe und kleine Boote auf dem Rhein sehen.

  h Die Häuser, Wohnungen und Geschäfte am Ufer des Rheins haben einen schonen Blick auf den Fluss.

TIPP

> If the subject of the verb does not start the sentence, it must go immediately after the verb.
>
> *Am Ende des Schultags **gehe** ich gern ins Café.*

2 Underline the subject in these sentences – it is not always the first thing.

  a Der Sommer ist meistens ziemlich heiß in Basel.

  b Trotz der Industrie finden wir die Stadt einfach super.

  c Es gibt vier offizielle Sprachen in der Schweiz.

  d In diesem nördlichen Teil der Schweiz spricht man immer Deutsch.

  e Der Schweizer Akzent und einige Wörter sind ganz anders als in Deutschland.

  f Abends haben die Basler eine große Auswahl an Freizeitaktivitäten.

3 Rewrite these sentences with the underlined phrase at the beginning.

  a Wir fahren <u>jeden Sommer</u> in die Schweiz. _____

  _____ .

  b Es gibt frische Luft <u>in den schönen Bergen</u>. _____

  _____ .

  c Man kann <u>den ganzen Tag</u> mit Freunden wandern.

  _____ .

  d Viele ausländische Touristen sehen die Schweiz <u>nur vom Reisebus</u>. _____

  _____ .

  e Die wunderschönen Seen sind <u>für Wassersport</u> sehr beliebt. _____

  _____ .

  f Meine Cousins und ich wollen <u>nächstes Jahr</u> auf einer Sommerrodelbahn fahren. _____

  _____ .

4 Place the verb in the correct position.

  a Mein älterer Bruder seit acht Jahren in Basel. (wohnt)

  _____

  b Jedes Wochenende im Winter er in die Berge zum Snowboarden. (geht)

  _____

  c Mit der Bahn und dem Bus die Fahrt etwa drei Stunden. (dauert)

  _____

  d Leider seine Freundin letzten Februar einen Unfall. (hatte)

  _____

  e Sie immer noch nicht gut laufen. (kann)

  _____

  f Meine Freundin und ich nächsten Winter mit ihm snowboarden. (wollen).

  _____

Time — Manner — Place

1 Rewrite these jumbled up sentences with the subject at the beginning.

a in einem Freizeitpark – mit einer Freundin – ich – arbeite – im Sommer

_____

_____ .

b im Sommer – Familien – an den Strand – fahren – mit ihren Kindern

_____

_____ .

c mit meinen Freunden – im Park – Rollschuh laufen – jedes Wochenende – kann – ich

_____

_____ .

d mit seiner Familie – mein englischer Brieffreund – eine Ferienwohnung – gemietet – hat – direkt am Meer – letzten August

_____

_____ .

e mit dem Rad – durch die Stadt – gefahren – wir – jeden Tag – sind

_____

_____ .

f arbeiten – ich – jeden Abend – im Café – sehr hart – muss

_____

_____ .

2 Using the information in Exercise 1, answer these questions. Start the answer with the part that is being asked for:

e.g. Wo arbeitest du im Sommer mit einer Freundin?
In einem Freizeitpark arbeite ich im Sommer mit einer Freundin.

a Mit wem fahren Familien im Sommer an den Strand?

_____ .

b Wann kannst du mit Freunden im Park Rollschuh laufen?

_____ .

c Was genau hat dein Brieffreund gemietet?

_____ .

d Wie seid ihr durch die Stadt gefahren und wann?

_____ .

e Wie oft musst du im Café arbeiten, und ist das hart?

_____ .

3 Write out these sentences with the correct word order. Remember 'time – manner – place' and 'verb second' rules.

a In Berlin, der größten Stadt Deutschlands, jetzt ungefähr 3,4 Millionen Menschen wohnen.

_____ .

b Meine Schwester studiert sehr hart in der Hochschule in Dortmund seit zwei Jahren.

_____ .

c Nach Innsbruck viele Touristen mit Reisebussen kommen im Juli.

_____ .

d Meine Brieffreundin wohnt in Bayern seit drei Jahren mit ihren Großeltern.

_____ .

e An der Ostsee man kann Strandkörbe für die Familie jeden Sommer mieten.

_____ .

f Der Physiker Albert Einstein zog nach Amerika 1932 mit seiner Familie.

_____ .

Joining sentences — coordinating conjunctions

Coordinating conjunctions are used to join two sentences of equal importance:

Max spielt gern Fußball. Seine Freundin treibt keinen Sport.

*Max spielt gern Fußball, **aber** seine Freundin treibt keinen Sport.*

Common coordinating conjunctions are:

und – and   *oder* – or
aber – but   *denn* – for, because

They do not affect the word order but are just added between the two clauses. There is usually a comma to separate the clauses.

1 Join the sentences using the coordinating conjunction in brackets.

a Bastian isst immer etwas Gesundes. Er fühlt sich viel besser deswegen. (und)

_____.

b Die Stadt Hamburg ist sehr groß. Sie ist trotzdem sehr freundlich. (aber)

_____.

c Ich bin ein paar Mal nach Berlin gefahren. Die Stadt gefällt mir sehr. (denn)

_____.

d Heute Abend gehen wir ins Kino. Vielleicht könnten wir zum Bowling gehen. (oder)

_____.

e Florian lernt jetzt Mathe. Nächstes Jahr wird er das nicht mehr machen. (aber)

_____.

2 Choose a suitable coordinating conjunction to complete the sentences. On separate paper, translate the sentences into English.

a Junge Leute wollen viel verdienen, _____ sie möchten nicht sehr hart arbeiten.

b Malena will Tierärztin werden, _____ sie hat Tiere so gern.

c In der Schule hat Karin nicht viel gearbeitet, _____ als Lehrling ist sie sehr fleißig.

d Ihr Bruder will Sport studieren, _____ vielleicht geht er zur Armee.

e Er arbeitet in einem Sportzentrum, _____ er bekommt kein Geld dafür.

f Das Leben in der Armee kann hart sein, _____ manchmal ist es sehr gefährlich.

Subordinating conjunctions

Subordinating conjunctions introduce a clause that adds more information to the main clause:

Max spielt in einem Verein. Er spielt gern Fußball.

*Max spielt in einem Verein, **weil** er gern Fußball spielt.*

Notice that the verb is at the end of the clause.

3 What kind of conjunctions are used in these sentences? Write C (coordinating) or S (subordinating).

a Im Sommer spielen wir oft Tennis, aber im Winter ist Basketball unser Lieblingssport. _____

b Ich spiele nicht Fußball, weil es für mich zu gefährlich ist. _____

c Er weiß noch nicht, ob er später Sportlehrer werden möchte. _____

d Man hat einen sicheren Job, aber es kann auch anstrengend sein. _____

e Gesundes Essen ist wichtig, wenn man viel Sport treibt. _____

f Miro hat drei Hamburger gegessen, obwohl er sie gar nicht mag. _____

g Sie haben ihm nicht geschmeckt, aber er hatte so großen Hunger. _____

h Ich hoffe, dass er keine Cola dazu getrunken hat. _____

4 Join these sentences using the subordinating conjunction in brackets.

a Ich esse jede Woche Fisch. Das ist gut für die Gesundheit. (weil)

_____

_____ .

b Wir fahren nicht gern Rad. Es regnet stark. (wenn)

_____

_____ .

c Ich bleibe noch eine Stunde hier. Du fährst mit Jens nach Hause. (während)

_____

_____ .

d Sie schreiben alles deutlich auf. Wir verstehen die Arbeit besser. (damit)

_____

_____ .

5 Join these sentences using the subordinating conjunction in brackets.

a Mir ist schlecht. Ich habe heute nicht zu viel gegessen. (obwohl)

_____ .

b Mein Freund ist nicht zufrieden. Er darf keine Süßigkeiten essen. (dass)

_____ .

c Alle sind aufgestanden. Er ist ins Zimmer gekommen. (als)

_____ .

d Ich warte unten im Wohnzimmer. Er zieht sich für die Party um. (während)

_____ .

e Er weiß nicht. Wir werden den Bus verpassen. (ob)

_____ .

6 Rewrite these sentences putting the subordinate clause at the beginning:

e.g. Ich fahre mit Freunden durch Europa, wenn ich mit der Schule fertig bin. *Wenn ich mit der Schule fertig **bin**, **fahre** ich mit Freunden durch Europa.*

a Die Schüler dürfen zu Hause bleiben, während die Heizung in der Schule nicht funktioniert.

_____ .

b Sie steht früh auf, obwohl sie heute keine Schule hat.

_____ .

c Du wirst zu viele Fehler machen, wenn du nicht aufpasst.

_____ .

d Alle hatten Angst, als die Direktorin plötzlich vor uns stand.

_____ .

Relative clauses

TIPP

Relative pronouns (see page 35) send the verb to the end of the clause, just like subordinating conjunctions. These **relative clauses** follow the same patterns as subordinate clauses:

*Das ist die Sportlerin, **die** viele Medaillen gewonnen **hat**.*

*Der Ball, **mit dem** wir jetzt **spielen**, ist viel zu alt.*

*Das Spiel, **das** gerade **anfängt**, sollte sehr gut sein.*

The relative pronouns are given in the following table.

	Masculine	Feminine	Neuter	Plural
Nom.	der	die	das	die
Acc.	den	die	das	die
Dat.	dem	der	dem	denen

1 Highlight the main verb in these sentences. Say what gender and case the underlined words are and whether they are singular or plural:

e.g. Ich habe die Arbeit mit diesem Kuli geschrieben. *masc., dat., sing.*

a Sie hat mir das Bild zum Geburtstag geschenkt.

_____

b Der Kuchen war für unsere Gäste. _____

c Unser Auto steht jetzt in der Werkstatt.

_____

d Unsere Katze sitzt auf dem Stuhl. _____

e Ich fahre mit diesen Freunden nach Wien.

_____

2 With the information from Exercise 1 (in the same order), use a relative pronoun to complete these sentences:

e.g. Das ist der Kuli, *mit dem ich die Arbeit geschrieben habe.*

a Ich liebe das Bild, _____
_____.

b Wir haben den Kuchen gegessen, _____
_____.

c Die Werkstatt, in _____
_____, hat eben angerufen.

d Gehört Ihnen der Stuhl, _____
_____?

e Ich gebe eine Party für die Freunde, _____
_____.

TIPP

If you refer to a whole clause rather than to a noun, use *was* (which) and send the verb to the end:

*Sie ist nicht zur Schule gekommen, **was** mich erstaunt **hat**.*

She didn't come to school, **which** surprised me.

3 Join these sentences using *was*.

a Er hat mir Blumen geschickt. Das hat mich sehr gefreut.

_____.

b Wir haben keinen Saft mehr. Das darf nicht wieder passieren.

_____.

c Anja hat eine schlechte Note in Mathe. Das ist kaum zu glauben.

_____.

d Der Hund hat deine Hausaufgaben gefressen. Das finde ich unglaublich.

_____.

4 Join these sentences using relative pronouns or *was*, as appropriate.

a Wir machen eine Stadtrundfahrt. Die Stadtrundfahrt dauert zwei Stunden.

_____.

b Der Bus war sehr unbequem. Das hat mich erstaunt.

_____.

c Ich habe mich mit einer netten Dame unterhalten. Sie kommt aus Dresden.

_____.

d Ich wusste nicht, wo Dresden war. Das hat mich geärgert.

_____.

e Die Dame zeigte mir eine Karte. Wir konnten Dresden auf dieser Karte finden.

_____.

Infinitives

TIPP

When two verbs are used together, the second verb is in the infinitive. The **infinitive** goes at the end of a clause, unless the other verb has been sent beyond it because of a subordinating conjunction or relative pronoun:

*Ich **werde** heute Abend nicht **fernsehen**,*

(infinitive at end)

*weil ich für eine Klassenarbeit **studieren muss**.*

(other verb at end)

1 Use the prompts to form complete sentences.

a Andrea – will – sich ansehen – einen Film – obwohl – muss – gehen – früh ins Bett

_____ .

_____ .

b in der Schule – man – darf – nicht laufen – weil – gefährlich

_____ .

_____ .

c morgen – ich – will – ausgehen – weil – das Wetter – wird – warm – sein

_____ .

_____ .

d Malik – muss – kaufen – neue Fußballschuhe – obwohl – er – kann – es sich nicht leisten

_____ .

_____ .

e Herr X – möchte – werden – Präsident – obwohl – das – nie – wird – geschehen

_____ .

_____ .

Past participles

TIPP

Similarly, **past participles** are normally at the end of the clause unless something has sent the auxiliary to the end:

*Max **hat** Fußball **gespielt**, während ich zu Hause **geschlafen habe**.*

2 Fill the gaps with words from the box.

a Wann hat er _____, dass der Bus schon _____ war?

b Sie haben nicht gut _____, weil sie nicht geübt _____ .

c Obwohl es nicht _____ hatte, _____ sie einen Regenschirm _____ .

d Der Film, den ihr _____ _____, hat drei Oscars _____ .

e Die Freunde, mit denen ich zur Party _____ _____, _____ spät nach Hause gekommen.

> abgefahren   gegangen   geregnet   gesehen
> gespielt   gewonnen   gewusst   habt   hat
> hatten   mitgenommen   sind   war

3 Correct the word order in these sentences.

a Der Wolf, der hat die Oma schon gefressen, will fressen auch Rotkäppchen.

_____ .

b Hast du gesehen den tollen Computer, den ich werde mir kaufen?

_____ .

c Wenn meine Eltern sind in Berlin angekommen, sie sollen mich anrufen.

_____ .

d Während ihr habt euch am Strand amüsiert, gelegen habe ich im Krankenhaus.

_____ .

e Was machen willst du, wenn hat der Regen aufgehört?

_____ .

Numbers, quantity, dates and times

Numbers

Numbers are mostly written as one word. Although you rarely have to write larger numbers in words, you need to be able to say them. The bold in the following list shows how there are slight variations to the patterns (e.g. *siebzehn*).

Notice that a comma is not used to separate large numbers – a space is used instead.

0	null	10	zehn	20	zwanzig	100	(ein)hundert
1	eins	11	elf	21	einundzwanzig	101	(ein)hunderteins
2	zwei	12	zwölf	22	zweiundzwanzig	159	(ein)hundertneunundfünfzig
3	drei	13	dreizehn	30	dreißig	570	fünfhundertsiebzig
4	vier	14	vierzehn	40	vierzig	1000	(ein)tausend
5	fünf	15	fünfzehn	50	fünfzig	1001	(ein)tausend(ein)eins
6	sechs	16	**sech**zehn	60	**sech**zig	5432	fünftausendvierhundertzweiunddreißig
7	sieben	17	**sieb**zehn	70	**sieb**zig	1 000 000	**eine M**illion
8	acht	18	achtzehn	80	achtzig	6 000 000	sechs Million**en**
9	neun	19	neunzehn	90	neunzig		

Telephone numbers are usually given in pairs of numbers (e.g. 24 36 ... = *vierundzwanzig sechsunddreißig ...*).

1 Write these numbers as you would say them.

a Telefon: 39 52 73 91 44 _____

_____

b 185 _____

c 7268 _____

d 9 876 543 _____

Prices are also written with a comma. The currency is the same in the singular and plural and it is said in between the numbers (as in English):

€ 1,50 (1,50 Euro) – *ein Euro fünfzig*

€ 10,90 (10,90 Euro) – *zehn Euro neunzig*

3 Write these prices as you would say them.

a € 16,40 _____

b € 27,80 _____

c € 1,95 _____

d CHF* 112,30 _____

e CHF 1506,50 _____

[*CHF = *Schweizer Franken* (normally just called *Franken*)]

German uses a comma instead of a decimal point:

1,5 – *eins Komma fünf* (1.5 – one point five)

2 Write these decimals as you would say them.

a 17,5% _____ Prozent

b 3,4 _____ Millionen Einwohner

c 99,9% _____

d 37,5°C _____ Grad Celsius

Ordinal numbers

TIPP

To form **ordinal numbers** (first, second etc.), add –t to numbers from 2 to 19, and –st to 20 and above. The exceptions are *erst–* (first), *dritt–* (third) and *siebt–* (seventh).

The words thus formed are now adjectives and need the appropriate endings (see Adjectives, pages 21–22): *der erste Tag*; *in der zehnten Klasse*; *zum hundertsten Mal*; *das einundzwanzigste Jahrhundert*.

1 Translate into German.

a the seventh day _____

b in the 11th class _____

c for the 20th time _____

d the 18th century _____

TIPP

To abbreviate ordinals, just add a dot after the number:

erst– *(1.)* first (1st)

zweit– *(2.)* second (2nd)

dritt– *(3.)* third (3rd)

zwanzigst– *(20.)* twentieth (20th)

2 Write these ordinals in abbreviated form:

e.g. das einundzwanzigste Jahrhundert
das 21. Jahrhundert

a mein sechzehnter Geburtstag

_____

b der vierundvierzigste Präsident

_____

c in der dreizehnten Klasse

_____

d am zwölften Mai

_____

TIPP

You can also use the ordinals to form fractions: 4 = *vier*; 4th = *viert–*; 1/4 = *ein Viertel*.

Note the use of a capital letter as this is now a noun.

There is one exception to this rule: 1/2 – *eine Hälfte* and *halb–* (*ein halber Liter*).

3 Write out these fractions as you would say them.

a 1/3 _____

b 1/5 _____

c 1/8 _____

d 1/20 _____

Quantity

TIPP

For a quantity of something, there is no need to say 'of': *ein Glas Milch, zwei Flaschen Cola, hundert Gramm Käse, viele Leute.*

4 Match the pairs.

1	hundert Gramm Wurst	a	a jar of jam
2	zwei Komma fünf Kilo Kartoffeln	b	a packet of noodles
3	ein Pfund (500 Gramm) Butter	c	lots of eggs
4	ein Liter Milch	d	2.5 kg potatoes
5	eine Flasche Limo	e	1 l milk
6	ein Glas Marmelade	f	100 g salami
7	ein Becher Jogurt	g	a box of chocolates
8	eine Packung Nudeln	h	a pot of yoghurt
9	eine Schachtel Pralinen	i	a bottle of lemonade
10	viele Eier	j	a pound (500 g) of butter

Dates

1 Write these dates as you would say them in German.

a (01/08) Der _____
ist der Schweizer Nationalfeiertag.

b (03/10) Der _____
ist der Tag der Deutschen Einheit.

c (26/10) Der _____
ist der österreichische Nationalfeiertag.

d (27/01) Der _____
ist Mozarts Geburtstag.

2 Answer these questions, writing the dates as you would say them.

a Wann ist der Valentinstag?

_____.

b An welchem Tag fiel die Berliner Mauer? (09/11/1989)

_____

c Wann ist Beethoven gestorben? (26/3/1827)

_____.

d Wann feiert man Weihnachten? (24–26/12)

_____

e Wann ist Silvester? (31/12)

_____.

f Wann hast du Geburtstag?

_____.

g Wann sind die Sommerferien?

_____.

3 Write these letter and postcard dates in full (as you would say them).

a (10/05) Hamburg, _____

b (15/06) Ulm, _____

c (21/07) Köln, _____

d (07/04) Wien, _____

e (30/09) Bern, _____

f (28/02) München, _____

4 Choose any four dates and say what happens on them. Remember to apply the correct word order.

e.g. *Am dritten August fahre ich mit Freunden nach Italien.*

a _____

_____.

b _____

_____.

c _____

_____.

d _____

_____.

Times

As in English, there are two ways of saying the **time**:

* The simplest way is just to use the hours and the minutes. For 24–hour clock times you must use this form:
    - *1.20 Uhr* (written) – *ein Uhr zwanzig* (spoken)
    - *2.45 Uhr* – *zwei Uhr fünfundvierzig*
    - *19.05 Uhr* – *neunzehn Uhr fünf*
* The other way is to use *nach* (past) and *vor* (to).

ein Uhr

fünf nach eins

zehn nach eins

Viertel nach eins

zwanzig nach eins

fünfundzwanzig nach eins

halb zwei

fünfundzwanzig vor zwei

zwanzig vor zwei

Viertel vor zwei

zehn vor zwei

fünf vor zwei

zwei Uhr

Mittag/Mitternacht

Pay particular attention to the way in which you say 'half past' the hour in German: it is halfway to the next hour: *halb **zwei*** means 'half past one'.

---

1 Write these times in the two different ways given in the Tipp. (You will have to change 24-hour times to 12-hour times for the second form):

e.g. 19.05 *neunzehn Uhr fünf – fünf nach sieben*

a 3.15 _____

_____

b 5.20 _____

_____

c 6.30 _____

_____

d 20.45 _____

_____

e 9.50 _____

_____

f 23.10 _____

_____

Note how to say 'it is' and 'at' a time:

*Wie spät **ist es**? Wie viel Uhr **ist es**?*
– **Es ist** 4 Uhr. – **It is** 4 o'clock.

***Wann** kommst du nach Hause?*
– **Um** 5 Uhr. – **At** 5 o'clock.

---

2 Answer the questions in German, writing the times in full as you would say them.

a Wie spät ist es jetzt?

_____.

b Wann stehst du normalerweise auf?

_____.

c Wann beginnt die erste Stunde?

_____.

d Um wie viel Uhr endet die Mittagspause?

_____.

e Wann gehst du unter der Woche ins Bett?

_____.

(See also pages 5 and 30 for practice of some common time phrases.)

Strong and irregular verbs

The following verb list includes most of the strong and mixed verbs you will need.

[NB: The 3rd person singular (er/sie/es/man) form is given in the verb table. This allows you to work out the other forms.]

[*These verbs use haben as the auxiliary if they have a direct object (e.g. Er hat den Bus gefahren).]

Infinitive	Present	Imperfect	Perfect	Meaning
beginnen	beginnt	begann	hat begonnen	to begin/start
bieten	bietet	bot	hat geboten	to offer
bleiben	bleibt	blieb	ist geblieben	to stay, remain
braten	brät	briet	hat gebraten	to roast
brechen	bricht	brach	hat gebrochen	to break
bringen	bringt	brachte	hat gebracht	to bring
denken	denkt	dachte	hat gedacht	to think
dürfen	darf	durfte	hat gedurft	to be allowed to
essen	isst	aß	hat gegessen	to eat
fahren	fährt	fuhr	ist* gefahren	to go (= travel)
fallen	fällt	fiel	ist gefallen	to fall
fliegen	fliegt	flog	ist* geflogen	to fly
frieren	friert	fror	hat gefroren	to freeze
geben	gibt	gab	hat gegeben	to give
gehen	geht	ging	ist gegangen	to go (= walk)
gewinnen	gewinnt	gewann	hat gewonnen	to win
haben	hat	hatte	hat gehabt	to have
halten	hält	hielt	hat gehalten	to hold, stop
heißen	heißt	hieß	hat geheißen	to be called
helfen	hilft	half	hat geholfen	to help
kennen	kennt	kannte	hat gekannt	to know (people)
kommen	kommt	kam	ist gekommen	to come
können	kann	konnte	hat gekonnt	to be able to, "can"
lassen	lässt	ließ	hat gelassen	to let, leave (s.th.)
laufen	läuft	lief	ist gelaufen	to run
leihen	leiht	lieh	hat geliehen	to lend
liegen	liegt	lag	hat gelegen	to lie (be lying down)

Infinitive	Present	Imperfect	Perfect	Meaning
mögen	mag	mochte	hat gemocht	*to like (to)*
müssen	muss	musste	hat gemusst	*to have to, "must"*
nehmen	nimmt	nahm	hat genommen	*to take*
reiten	reitet	ritt	ist* geritten	*to ride (horse)*
rufen	ruft	rief	hat gerufen	*to call (= shout)*
scheinen	scheint	schien	hat geschienen	*to shine*
schlafen	schläft	schlief	hat geschlafen	*to sleep*
schlagen	schlägt	schlug	hat geschlagen	*to hit*
schließen	schließ	schloss	hat geschlossen	*to close*
schneiden	schneidet	schnitt	hat geschnitten	*to cut*
schreiben	schreibt	schrieb	hat geschrieben	*to write*
schreien	schreit	schrie	hat geschrie(e)n	*to shout, scream*
schwimmen	schwimmt	schwamm	ist geschwommen	*to swim*
sehen	sieht	sah	hat gesehen	*to see*
sein	ist	war	ist gewesen	*to be*
senden	sendet	sandte	hat gesandt	*to send*
sitzen	sitzt	saß	hat gesessen	*to sit (= be sitting)*
sollen	soll	sollte	hat gesollt	*to be supposed to, "should"*
sprechen	spricht	sprach	hat gesprochen	*to speak*
springen	springt	sprang	ist gesprungen	*to jump*
stehen	steht	stand	hat gestanden	*to stand*
steigen	steigt	stieg	ist gestiegen	*to climb*
sterben	stirbt	starb	ist gestorben	*to die*
treffen	trifft	traf	hat getroffen	*to meet (by intention)*
trinken	trinkt	trank	hat getrunken	*to drink*
tun	tut	tat	hat getan	*to do*
verlieren	verliert	verlor	hat verloren	*to lose*
waschen	wäscht	wusch	hat gewaschen	*to wash*
werden	wird	wurde	ist geworden	*to become, get*
werfen	wirft	warf	hat geworfen	*to throw*
wiegen	wiegt	wog	hat gewogen	*to weigh*
wissen	weiß	wusste	hat gewusst	*to know (facts)*
wollen	will	wollte	hat gewollt	*to want to*
ziehen	zieht	zog	hat gezogen	*to pull*

Separable and inseparable compounds of the strong and mixed verbs (e.g. **beschreiben**, **aufstehen**) follow the same pattern as the root verb In some cases, the auxiliary verb (in the perfect tense) is different from that of the root verb. In the following list, the root verb is in bold.

Infinitive	Present	Imperfect	Perfect	Meaning
abfahren	fährt ab	fuhr ab	ist abgefahren	to depart
abschließen	schließt ab	schloss ab	hat abgeschlossen	to lock (up)
anhalten	hält an	hielt an	hat angehalten	to stop (vehicles)
ankommen	kommt an	kam an	ist angekommen	to arrive
annehmen	nimmt an	nahm an	hat angenommen	to accept
sich ansehen	sieht sich an	sah sich an	hat sich angesehen	to watch
anspringen	springt an	sprang an	ist angesprungen	to start (cars)
sich anziehen	zieht sich an	zog sich an	hat sich angezogen	to get dressed
aufstehen	steht auf	stand auf	ist aufgestanden	to get up, stand up
ausgehen	geht aus	ging aus	ist ausgegangen	to go out
auskommen	kommt aus	kam aus	ist ausgekommen	to get on (with)
aussteigen	steigt aus	stieg aus	ist ausgestiegen	to get off
bekommen	bekommt	bekam	hat bekommen	to receive, get
beschreiben	beschreibt	beschrieb	hat beschrieben	to describe
einschlafen	schläft ein	schlief ein	ist eingeschlafen	to go to sleep
einsteigen	steigt ein	stieg ein	ist eingestiegen	to get on
fernsehen	sieht fern	sah fern	hat ferngesehen	to watch TV
mitnehmen	nimmt mit	nahm mit	hat mitgenommen	to take (with you)
umsteigen	steigt um	stieg um	ist umgestiegen	to change (e.g. trains)
umziehen	zieht um	zog um	ist umgezogen	to move house
sich umziehen	zieht sich um	zog sich um	hat sich umgezogen	to get changed
unterschreiben	unterschreibt	unterschrieb	hat unterschrieben	to sign
verbieten	verbietet	verbot	hat verboten	to forbid
verbringen	verbringt	verbrachte	hat verbracht	to spend (= time)
verlassen	verlässt	verließ	hat verlassen	to leave (place)
verstehen	versteht	verstand	hat verstanden	to understand
vorbeigehen	geht vorbei	ging vorbei	ist vorbeigegangen	to go past (on foot)
weggehen	geht weg	ging weg	ist weggegangen	to go away
wegwerfen	wirft weg	warf weg	hat weggeworfen	to throw away
zunehmen	nimmt zu	nahm zu	hat zugenommen	to grow (= get bigger)
zurückkommen	kommt zurück	kam zurück	ist zurückgekommen	to return, come/go back

Verb guide

The following pages provide a reference guide with an example of different types of verb in all the main tenses and verb forms.

Weak verbs

Infinitive	spielen	to play
Stem	spiel-	–
Present tense	ich spiele du spielst er/sie/es spielt wir spielen ihr spielt Sie spielen sie spielen	I play you (familiar) play he/she/it plays we play you (familiar pl.) play you (polite) play they play
Imperfect tense	ich spielte du spieltest er/sie/es spielte wir spielten ihr spieltet Sie spielten sie spielten	I played you (familiar) played he/she/it played we played you (familiar pl.) played you (polite) played they played
Perfect tense	ich habe gespielt du hast gespielt er/sie/es hat gespielt wir haben gespielt ihr habt gespielt Sie haben gespielt sie haben gespielt	I (have) played you (familiar) (have) played he/she/it (has) played we (have) played you (familiar pl.) (have) played you (polite) (have) played they (have) played
Pluperfect tense	ich hatte gespielt du hattest gespielt er/sie/es hatte gespielt wir hatten gespielt ihr hattet gespielt Sie hatten gespielt sie hatten gespielt	I (had) played you (familiar) (had) played he/she/it (has) played we (had) played you (familiar pl.) (had) played you (polite) (had) played they (had) played

Future tense	ich werde spielen du wirst spielen er/sie/es wird spielen wir werden spielen ihr werdet spielen Sie werden spielen sie werden spielen	I will play you (familiar) will play he/she/it will play we will play you (familiar pl.) will play you (polite) will play they will play
Conditional	ich würde spielen du würdest spielen er/sie/es würde spielen wir würden spielen ihr würdet spielen Sie würden spielen sie würden spielen	I would play you (familiar) would play he/she/it would play we would play you (familiar pl.) would play you (polite) would play they would play
Imperative	spiel! spielt! spielen Sie!	play!

Strong verbs (with haben)

Infinitive	nehmen	to take
Stem	nehm–	–
Present tense	ich nehme	I take
	du nimmst	you (familiar) take
	er/sie/es nimmt	he/she/it takes
	wir nehmen	we take
	ihr nehmt	you (familiar pl.) take
	Sie nehmen	you (polite) take
	sie nehmen	they take
Imperfect tense	ich nahm	I took
	du nahmst	you (familiar) took
	er/sie/es nahm	he/she/it took
	wir nahmen	we took
	ihr nahmt	you (familiar pl.) took
	Sie nahmen	you (polite) took
	sie nahmen	they took
Perfect tense	ich habe genommen	I took/have taken
	du hast genommen	you (familiar) took/have taken
	er/sie/es hat genommen	he/she/it took/has taken
	wir haben genommen	we took/have taken
	ihr habt genommen	you (familiar pl.) took/have taken
	Sie haben genommen	you (polite) took/have taken
	sie haben genommen	they took/have taken
Pluperfect tense	ich hatte genommen	I had taken
	du hattest genommen	you (familiar) had taken
	er/sie/es hatte genommen	he/she/it had taken
	wir hatten genommen	we had taken
	ihr hattet genommen	you (familiar pl.) had taken
	Sie hatten genommen	you (polite) had taken
	sie hatten genommen	they had taken

Future tense	ich werde nehmen	I will take
	du wirst nehmen	you (familiar) will take
	er/sie/es wird nehmen	he/she/it will take
	wir werden nehmen	we will take
	ihr werdet nehmen	you (familiar pl.) will take
	Sie werden nehmen	you (polite) will take
	sie werden nehmen	they will take
Conditional	ich würde nehmen	I would take
	du würdest nehmen	you (familiar) would take
	er/sie/es würde nehmen	he/she/it would take
	wir würden nehmen	we would take
	ihr würdet nehmen	you (familiar pl.) would take
	Sie würden nehmen	you (polite) would take
	sie würden nehmen	they would take
Imperative	nimm!	take!
	nehmt!	
	nehmen Sie!	

Strong verbs (with *sein*)

Infinitive	fahren	to go
Stem	fahr–	–

Present tense		
	ich fahre	I go
	du fährst	you (familiar) go
	er/sie/es fährt	he/she/it goes
	wir fahren	we go
	ihr fahrt	you (familiar pl.) go
	Sie fahren	you (polite) go
	sie fahren	they go

Imperfect tense		
	ich fuhr	I went
	du fuhrst	you (familiar) went
	er/sie/es fuhr	he/she/it went
	wir fuhren	we went
	ihr fuhrt	you (familiar pl.) went
	Sie fuhren	you (polite) went
	sie fuhren	they went

Perfect tense		
	ich bin gefahren	I went/have gone
	du bist gefahren	you (familiar) went/have gone
	er/sie/es ist gefahren	he/she/it went/has gone
	wir sind gefahren	we went/have gone
	ihr seid gefahren	you (familiar pl.) went/have gone
	Sie sind gefahren	you (polite) went/have gone
	sie sind gefahren	they went/have gone

Pluperfect tense		
	ich war gefahren	I had gone
	du warst gefahren	you (familiar) had gone
	er/sie/es war gefahren	he/she/it had gone
	wir waren gefahren	we had gone
	ihr wart gefahren	you (familiar pl.) had gone
	Sie waren gefahren	you (polite) had gone
	sie waren gefahren	they had gone

Future tense		
	ich werde fahren	I will go
	du wirst fahren	you (familiar) will go
	er/sie/es wird fahren	he/she/it will go
	wir werden fahren	we will go
	ihr werdet fahren	you (familiar pl.) will go
	Sie werden fahren	you (polite) will go
	sie werden fahren	they will go

Conditional		
	ich würde fahren	I would go
	du würdest fahren	you (familiar) would go
	er/sie/es würde fahren	he/she/it would go
	wir würden fahren	we would go
	ihr würdet fahren	you (familiar pl.) would go
	Sie würden fahren	you (polite) would go
	sie würden fahren	they would go

Imperative		
	fahr!	go!
	fahrt!	
	fahren Sie!	

Separable and inseparable verbs (both can be weak or strong)

	Separable	Inseparable
Infinitive	einkaufen – *to shop*	beschreiben – *to describe*
Present tense	ich kaufe ein du kaufst ein er/sie/es kauft ein wir kaufen ein ihr kauft ein Sie kaufen ein sie kaufen ein	ich beschreibe du beschreibst er/sie/es beschreibt wir beschreiben ihr beschreibt Sie beschreiben sie beschreiben
Imperfect tense	ich kaufte ein du kauftest ein er/sie/es kaufte ein wir kauften ein ihr kauftet ein Sie kauften ein sie kauften ein	ich beschrieb du beschriebst er/sie/es beschrieb wir beschrieben ihr beschriebt Sie beschrieben sie beschrieben
Perfect tense	ich habe eingekauft du hast eingekauft er/sie/es hat eingekauft wir haben eingekauft ihr habt eingekauft Sie haben eingekauft sie haben eingekauft	ich habe beschrieben du hast beschrieben er/sie/es hat beschrieben wir haben beschrieben ihr habt beschrieben Sie haben beschrieben sie haben beschrieben
Pluperfect tense	ich hatte eingekauft du hattest eingekauft er/sie/es hatte eingekauft wir hatten eingekauft ihr hattet eingekauft Sie hatten eingekauft sie hatten eingekauft	ich hatte beschrieben du hattest beschrieben er/sie/es hatte beschrieben wir hatten beschrieben ihr hattet beschrieben Sie hatten beschrieben sie hatten beschrieben
Future tense	ich werde einkaufen du wirst einkaufen er/sie/es wird einkaufen wir werden einkaufen ihr werdet einkaufen Sie werden einkaufen sie werden einkaufen	ich werde beschreiben du wirst beschreiben er/sie/es wird beschreiben wir werden beschreiben ihr werdet beschreiben Sie werden beschreiben sie werden beschreiben
Conditional	ich würde einkaufen du würdest einkaufen er/sie/es würde einkaufen wir würden einkaufen ihr würdet einkaufen Sie würden einkaufen sie würden einkaufen	ich würde beschreiben du würdest beschreiben er/sie/es würde beschreiben wir würden beschreiben ihr würdet beschreiben Sie würden beschreiben sie würden beschreiben
Imperative	kauf ein! kauft ein! kaufen Sie ein!	beschreib! beschreibt! beschreiben Sie!

Reflexive verbs (this one is strong, but many are weak)

Infinitive	sich waschen	to get washed
Present tense	ich wasche mich	I get washed
	du wäschst dich	you (familiar) get washed
	er/sie/es wäscht sich	he/she/it gets washed
	wir waschen uns	we get washed
	ihr wascht euch	you (familiar pl.) get washed
	Sie waschen sich	you (polite) get washed
	sie waschen sich	they get washed
Imperfect tense	ich wusch mich	I got washed
	du wuschst dich	you (familiar) got washed
	er/sie/es wusch sich	he/she/it got washed
	wir wuschen uns	we got washed
	ihr wuscht euch	you (familiar pl.) got washed
	Sie wuschen sich	you (polite) got washed
	sie wuschen sich	they got washed
Perfect tense	ich habe mich gewaschen	I (have) got washed
	du hast dich gewaschen	you (familiar) (have) got washed
	er/sie/es hat sich gewaschen	he/she/it (has) got washed
	wir haben uns gewaschen	we (have) got washed
	ihr habt euch gewaschen	you (familiar pl.) (have) got washed
	Sie haben sich gewaschen	you (polite) (have) got washed
	sie haben sich gewaschen	they (have) got washed
Pluperfect tense	ich hatte mich gewaschen	I had got washed
	du hattest dich gewaschen	you (familiar) had got washed
	er/sie/es hatte sich gewaschen	he/she/it had got washed
	wir hatten uns gewaschen	we had got washed
	ihr hattet euch gewaschen	you (familiar pl.) had got washed
	Sie hatten sich gewaschen	you (polite) had got washed
	sie hatten sich gewaschen	they had got washed

Future tense	ich werde mich waschen	I will get washed
	du wirst dich waschen	you (familiar) will get washed
	er/sie/es wird sich waschen	he/she/it will get washed
	wir werden uns waschen	we will get washed
	ihr werdet euch waschen	you (familiar pl.) will get washed
	Sie werden sich waschen	you (polite) will get washed
	sie werden sich waschen	they will get washed
Conditional	ich würde mich waschen	I would get washed
	du würdest dich waschen	you (familiar) would get washed
	er/sie/es würde sich waschen	he/she/it would get washed
	wir würden uns waschen	we would get washed
	ihr würdet euch waschen	you (familiar pl.) would get washed
	Sie würden sich waschen	you (polite) would get washed
	sie würden sich waschen	they would get washed
Imperative	wasch dich!	get washed!
	wascht euch!	
	waschen Sie sich!	

Modal verbs

Infinitive		dürfen	können	mögen	müssen	sollen	wollen
Meaning		*to be allowed to*	*to be able to*	*to like to*	*to have to*	*to be supposed to*	*to want to*
Present tense	ich	darf	kann	mag	muss	soll	will
	du	darfst	kannst	magst	musst	sollst	willst
	er/sie/es	darf	kann	mag	muss	soll	will
	wir	dürfen	können	mögen	müssen	sollen	wollen
	ihr	dürft	könnt	mögt	müsst	sollt	wollt
	Sie/sie	dürfen	können	mögen	müssen	sollen	wollen
Imperfect tense	ich	durfte	konnte	mochte	musste	sollte	wollte
	du	durftest	konntest	mochtest	musstest	solltest	wolltest
	er/sie/es	durfte	konnte	mochte	musste	sollte	wollte
	wir	durften	konnten	mochten	mussten	sollten	wollten
	ihr	durftet	konntet	mochtet	musstet	solltet	wolltet
	Sie/sie	durften	konnten	mochten	mussten	sollten	wollten
Perfect tense	ich	habe gedurft	habe gekonnt	habe gemocht	habe gemusst	habe gesollt	habe gewollt
	du	hast gedurft	hast gekonnt	hast gemocht	hast gemusst	hast gesollt	hast gewollt
	er/sie/es	hat gedurft	hat gekonnt	hat gemocht	hat gemusst	hat gesollt	hat gewollt
	wir	haben gedurft	haben gekonnt	haben gemocht	haben gemusst	haben gesollt	haben gewollt
	ihr	habt gedurft	habt gekonnt	habt gemocht	habt gemusst	habt gesollt	habt gewollt
	Sie/sie	haben gedurft	haben gekonnt	haben gemocht	haben gemusst	haben gesollt	haben gewollt
Pluperfect tense	ich	hatte gedurft	hatte gekonnt	hatte gemocht	hatte gemusst	hatte gesollt	hatte gewollt
	du	hattest gedurft	hattest gekonnt	hattest gemocht	hattest gemusst	hattest gesollt	hattest gewollt
	er/sie/es	hatte gedurft	hatte gekonnt	hatte gemocht	hatte gemusst	hatte gesollt	hatte gewollt
	wir	hatten gedurft	hatten gekonnt	hatten gemocht	hatten gemusst	hatten gesollt	hatten gewollt
	ihr	hattet gedurft	hattet gekonnt	hattet gemocht	hattet gemusst	hattet gesollt	hattet gewollt
	Sie/sie	hatten gedurft	hatten gekonnt	hatten gemocht	hatten gemusst	hatten gesollt	hatten gewollt
Future tense	ich	werde dürfen	werde können	werde mögen	werde müssen	werde sollen	werde wollen
	du	wirst dürfen	wirst können	wirst mögen	wirst müssen	wirst sollen	wirst wollen
	er/sie/es	wird dürfen	wird können	wird mögen	wird müssen	wird sollen	wird wollen
	wir	werden dürfen	werden können	werden mögen	werden müssen	werden sollen	werden wollen
	ihr	werdet dürfen	werdet können	werdet mögen	werdet müssen	werdet sollen	werdet wollen
	Sie/sie	werden dürfen	werden können	werden mögen	werden müssen	werden sollen	werden wollen
Conditional	ich	würde dürfen	würde können	würde mögen	würde müssen	würde sollen	würde wollen
	du	würdest dürfen	würdest können	würdest mögen	würdest müssen	würdest sollen	würdest wollen
	er/sie/es	würde dürfen	würde können	würde mögen	würde müssen	würde sollen	würde wollen
	wir	würden dürfen	würden können	würden mögen	würden müssen	würden sollen	würden wollen
	ihr	würdet dürfen	würdet können	würdet mögen	würdet müssen	würdet sollen	würdet wollen
	Sie/sie	würden dürfen	würden können	würden mögen	würden müssen	würden sollen	würden wollen

Auxiliary verbs: *haben, sein, werden*			
Infinitive	haben	sein	werden
Meaning	*to have*	*to be*	*to become*
Present tense	ich habe du hast er/sie/es hat	ich bin du bist er/sie/es ist	ich werde du wirst er/sie/es wird
	wir haben ihr habt Sie haben sie haben	wir sind ihr seid Sie sind sie sind	wir werden ihr werdet Sie werden sie werden
Imperfect tense	ich hatte du hattest er/sie/es hatte	ich war du warst er/sie/es war	ich wurde du wurdest er/sie/es wurde
	wir hatten ihr hattet Sie hatten sie hatten	wir waren ihr wart Sie waren sie waren	wir wurden ihr wurdet Sie wurden sie wurden
Perfect tense	ich habe gehabt du hast gehabt er/sie/es hat gehabt	ich bin gewesen du bist gewesen er/sie/es ist gewesen	ich bin geworden du bist geworden er/sie/es ist geworden
	wir haben gehabt ihr habt gehabt Sie haben gehabt sie haben gehabt	wir sind gewesen ihr seid gewesen Sie sind gewesen sie sind gewesen	wir sind geworden ihr seid geworden Sie sind geworden sie sind geworden
Pluperfect tense	ich hatte gehabt du hattest gehabt er/sie/es hatte gehabt	ich war gewesen du warst gewesen er/sie/es war gewesen	ich war geworden du warst geworden er/sie/es war geworden
	wir hatten gehabt ihr hattet gehabt Sie hatten gehabt sie hatten gehabt	wir waren gewesen ihr wart gewesen Sie waren gewesen sie waren gewesen	wir waren geworden ihr wart geworden Sie waren geworden sie waren geworden
Future tense	ich werde haben du wirst haben er/sie/es wird haben	ich werde sein du wirst sein er/sie/es wird sein	ich werde werden du wirst werden er/sie/es wird werden
	wir werden haben ihr werdet haben Sie werden haben sie werden haben	wir werden sein ihr werdet sein Sie werden sein sie werden sein	wir werden werden ihr werdet werden Sie werden werden sie werden werden
Conditional	ich würde haben du würdest haben er/sie/es würde haben	ich würde sein du würdest sein er/sie/es würde sein	ich würde werden du würdest werden er/sie/es würde werden
	wir würden haben ihr würdet haben Sie würden haben sie würden haben	wir würden sein ihr würdet sein Sie würden sein sie würden sein	wir würden werden ihr würdet werden Sie würden werden sie würden werden
Imperative	hab! habt! haben Sie!	sei! seid! seien Sie!	werde! werdet! werden Sie!

(page 4)

1 (pronouns underlined, **nouns bold**)

a Ich habe ein tolles **Zimmer**, wo ich meine **Hausaufgaben** mache.

b Mein **Bruder** hat ein ziemlich kleines **Zimmer** mit einem **Einbauschrank**.

c Er hört dort **Musik** und ich spiele mit ihm am **Computer**.

d Wir haben eine große **Küche**, wo ich immer frühstücke.

e Wir haben auch einen schönen **Garten** mit vielen **Blumen**.

f Wir haben zwei **Hunde**. Jeden **Tag** gehe ich mit ihnen spazieren.

g Nach dem **Abendessen** sehe ich meistens ein bisschen fern.

2 **a** Mein Bruder hat viele Filme.

b Ich sehe deine Schwester im Park.

c Machst du deine Hausaufgaben?

d Unsere Großeltern haben ein schönes Haus.

e Thomas hat sein neues Buch schon gelesen.

f Wo ist dein Zimmer?

g Normalerweise kommen Mutti und Vati um 18 Uhr nach Hause.

h Nach der Schule sehen mein Bruder und ich fern.

3 **a** mein, **b** berühmter, **c** unsere, **d** mein, **e** keine, **f** eine

4 open-ended

(page 5)

1 **a** Meine Schwestern haben viele Computerspiele.

b Ich sehe deinen Bruder in der Sporthalle.

c Warum macht ihr eure Hausaufgaben nicht?

d Unsere Freunde werden ein schönes Haus kaufen.

e Ich habe das große Buch schon gelesen.

f Hat Max diese CD schon gehört?

g Im Sommer spiele ich sehr gern Tennis.

h Zum Geburtstag hat mir meine Tante eine Jacke gegeben.

i Heike fährt in die Stadt und kauft sich einen Pullover.

j Sie ist ins Kaufhaus gegangen, hat aber nichts Passendes gefunden.

2 **a** letzte Woche, **b** nächsten Dienstag, **c** nächsten Monat, **d** letzten Freitag, **e** letztes Jahr

3 **a** for my father, **b** through the town, **c** without his bike, **d** along the main road, **e** against the wall, **f** round the car park

4 **a** Bitte, stell die Bücher auf den Tisch!

b Das Schwimmbad ist neben dem Stadion am Stadtrand.

c Wir gehen gleich in die Sporthalle.

d Es ist schwierig, wenn man immer im Restaurant essen muss.

e Welche Sportart möchtest du ausprobieren?

f Die meisten Menschen werden beim Himalaya an die hohen Berge denken.

(page 6)

1 **a** the title of the book, **b** the teacher's voice, **c** my mother's car, **d** the tennis player of the year, **e** the beginning of the exams

2 Masculine and neuter nouns which have one syllable add *-es* in the genitive singular. Add just *-s* in the genitive singular for masculine and neuter nouns with two or more syllables. Feminine and plural nouns do not change in the genitive case.

3 **a** the bike of my sister = das Rad meiner Schwester

b the house of his grandparents = das Haus seiner Großeltern

c the motto of this school = das Motto dieser Schule

d he has the computer of his brother = er hat den Computer seines Bruders

e in the car of my friend = mit dem Wagen meines Freundes/meiner Freundin

4 **a** außerhalb, **b** wegen, **c** während, **d** Trotz, **e** statt

(page 7)

1 **1** d – Der Koch gab der Katze einen Fisch. **2** f – Frau Fischer kauft mir eine Katze. **3** a – Ich erzähle den Kindern eine Geschichte. **4** c – Er schrieb dem Direktor einen Brief. **5** b – Schickst du deinem Freund eine E-Mail? **6** e – Gib der Dame deine E-Mail-Adresse!

2 **a** with my friends, **b** opposite the bank, **c** after an hour, **d** out of the garden, **e** at our grandma's house, **f** my (girl)friend's mother

3 **a** Das Restaurant war hinter dem Rathaus.

b Als Skilehrer bin ich stundenlang auf den Pisten.

c Lies diese Broschüre über gesundes Essen!

d Wir stehen vor dem Kino und warten.

e Ich freue mich auf die Sommerferien.

f Sein Foto hängt an <u>der Wand</u>.

4 a Der blaue Rock passt <u>meiner Schwester</u> nicht. – The blue skirt doesn't suit/fit my sister.

b Ich glaube <u>dir</u> nicht! – I don't believe you.

c Wir dankten <u>dem Gruppenleiter</u>. – We thanked the group leader.

d Kannst du <u>mir</u> bitte helfen? – Can you please help me?

e Er folgte <u>den Spielern</u> ins Stadion. – He followed the players into the stadium.

f Diese Geschichte gefällt <u>mir</u> nicht. – I don't like this story.

(page 8)

1 (nouns) **a** profession, **d** receptionist, **f** size, **g** main road, **h** ICT, **j** sleeping bag, **l** onion

2 a die Fabrik, **b** das Gemüse, **c** die Prüfung, **d** das Mädchen, **e** die Schule, **f** der Bäcker, **g** die Seekrankheit, **h** die Nation, **i** das Zentrum, **j** die Verkäuferin, **k** die Einladung, **l** die Freundschaft

3 (underlined words) **a** Vater, **b** Geburtstag, **c** Krankenhaus, **d** Ingenieurin, **e** Hase, **f** Restaurant, **g** Geige, **h** Skigebiet

(page 9)

1 open-ended

2 a die Meerschweinchen, **b** die Karten, **c** die Fächer, **d** die Schläger, **e** die Babys, **f** die Geburtstage, **g** die Hügel, **h** die Köchinnen, **i** die Gasthäuser, **j** die Füße, **k** die Zeitungen

3 a der Bahnhof, **b** die Digitalkamera, **c** der Stiefel, **d** die Übernachtung, **e** der Turnschuh, **f** die Verkäuferin, **g** das Würstchen, **h** die Katze, **i** das Datum, **j** der Autofahrer, **k** das Jugendzentrum

4 a mit den Hunden, **b** aus den Häusern, **c** in den Schulen, **d** von diesen Mädchen, **e** hinter den Hotels

(page 10)

1 a Hast du den <u>Alten</u> gesehen? (A)

b Die <u>Armen</u> haben heute eine Prüfung. (N)

c Wir fahren mit <u>Verwandten</u> nach Berlin. (D)

d Er möchte eine <u>Reiche</u> kennenlernen. (A)

e Ich kenne viele <u>Deutsche</u>. (A)

f Er hat dem <u>Beamten</u> seinen Pass gezeigt. (D)

2 a wichtig – important, **b** interessant – interesting, **c** groß – big/tall, **d** klein – small, **e** tot – dead

3 a ein Bekannter, **b** die Deutschen, **c** ein Kranker, **d** das Weiße, **e** eine Fremde, **f** die Kluge

4 a Der Student(–) hat seinem Kamerad<u>en</u> eine Postkarte geschickt.

b Er gibt Herr<u>n</u> Büddig sein Heft.

c Sein Neffe(–) ist der Sohn eines Kolleg<u>en</u>.

d Unter den Tourist<u>en</u> haben wir einen berühmten Mensch<u>en</u> gesehen.

e Im Zoo haben wir einen Bär<u>en</u>, viele Affe<u>n</u> und einen Löwe<u>n</u> gefüttert.

f Der Junge(–) hat den Name<u>n</u> eines anderen Studenten geschrieben.

(page 11)

1

der	<u>die</u>	das	<u>die</u>
<u>den</u>	die	<u>das</u>	die
des	der	<u>des</u>	der
<u>dem</u>	<u>der</u>	dem	<u>den</u>

2 a ein, eines, **b** Eine, **c** einer, einem, **d** kein, **e** keinen, keine

3 a Sie ist Deutsche. **b** Herr Schmidt ist Bäcker. **c** Ich spiele Klarinette. **d** Hast du/Haben Sie Fieber? **e** Sie hat Kopfschmerzen.

(page 12)

1

mein	<u>meine</u>	mein	meine
<u>meinen</u>	meine	mein	meine
<u>meines</u>	meiner	meines	meiner
<u>meinem</u>	meiner	meinem	meinen

ihr	<u>ihre</u>	<u>ihr</u>	ihre
<u>ihren</u>	ihre	<u>ihr</u>	ihre
<u>ihres</u>	ihrer	<u>ihres</u>	ihrer
<u>ihrem</u>	ihrer	<u>ihrem</u>	ihren

unser	<u>unsere</u>	<u>unser</u>	unsere
<u>unseren</u>	unsere	unser	unsere
<u>unseres</u>	unserer	unseres	unserer
<u>unserem</u>	unserer	unserem	unseren

euer	<u>eure</u>	<u>euer</u>	eure
euren	eure	euer	eure
<u>eures</u>	eurer	<u>eures</u>	eurer
<u>eurem</u>	eurer	eurem	euren

2 a mein Haus, **b** seine Mutter, **c** deine Freunde, **d** ihre Eltern, **e** unsere Schule, **f** ihr Geld, **g** Ihr Job/Beruf, **h** ihr Spielzeug, **i** sein Teppich, **j** eure Bücher

3 open-ended

(page 13)
1

dieser	diese	dieses	diese
diesen	diese	dieses	diese
dieses	dieser	dieses	dieser
diesem	dieser	diesem	diesen

jener	jene	jenes	jene
jenen	jene	jenes	jene
jenes	jener	jenes	jener
jenem	jener	jenem	jenen

jeder	jede	jedes
jeden	jede	jedes
jedes	jeder	jedes
jedem	jeder	jedem

2
a Welche Produkte sind billig?

b Welche Sportart ziehst du vor?

c Welchen Film habt ihr gestern gesehen?

d Mit welchem Bus fahren wir in die Stadt?

e In welchen Geschäften kaufst du am liebsten ein?

f Welches Kind hat die beste Stimme?

g Aus welchem Grund sagst du das?

h Durch welchen Eingang sind Sie gekommen?

(page 14)
1
1 through, **i** durch, A

2 on, **f** auf, D

3 because of, **b** wegen, G

4 without, **j** ohne, A

5 between, **h** zwischen, D

6 instead of, **a** statt, G

7 by, **l** von, D

8 before, **k** vor, D

9 after, **e** nach, D

10 into, **g** in, A

11 in, **d** nach, D

2 a für seine Schwester, **b** gegen einen Baum, **c** die Autobahn entlang, **d** um die Stadt, **e** durch die Tür, **f** ohne ihre Freunde/Freundinnen, **g** gegen die Jungen, **h** um den Tisch

3 open-ended

(page 15)
1 a bei, **b** aus, **c** Seit, **d** vor/nach, **e** zu, **f** neben/hinter/über/unter/vor, **g** mit, **h** nach, **i** Außer, **j** von

2 a beim, **b** zum, **c** zur, **d** vom, (bis) zum, **e** vom, **f** Beim

3 a There you are at last! I've been waiting here in the cold for 10 minutes.

b I'd been waiting for an hour in the cold and my sister still hadn't arrived.

c We've been learning German for three years.

d We'd been learning German for three years and could understand quite a lot.

e She's been a singer in a band for four years.

f She'd been a singer for four years, but had never sung in a band.

(page 16)
1 a A, D, **b** D, A, **c** D, A, **d** A, D, **e** A, D, **f** D, A, **g** A, D, **h** A, D, **i** D, A

2 a am, **b** ins, **c** ans, **d** ins, **e** im, **f** Am

(page 17)
3 a im, **b** die, **c** im, der, **d** die, im, **e** das, **f** seinem, **g** die, **h** im, ins

4 a We went into the town centre. We drove around in the town centre.

b He sat down by the window. He is sitting by the window.

c A plane flies over school every 10 minutes. The planes are so loud when they are directly above the school.

d Our cat sleeps under my bed. Every night at 10 o'clock the cat creeps under my bed.

5 a den, **b** dem, im, **c** meinem, **d** das, die, **e** der, einem, **f** die, den

6 1 prepositions, 2 movement, 3 accusative, 4 *den*, 5 into, 6 position, 7 place, 8 dative, 9 *dem*, 10 another, 11 choice, 12 always

(page 18)
1

außerhalb	outside
statt	instead of
trotz	despite/in spite of
während	during
wegen	because of

2 a Because of the rain we can't do any sport.

b Instead of our teacher, the headmaster taught us German.

c During the party my parents were at neighbours'.

d We live about five kilometres outside the town.

e During the hike it started to snow..

f Despite her cold she went swimming.

3 **Accusative only:** durch, entlang, für, gegen, ohne, um, wider

Dative only: aus, außer, bei, gegenüber, mit, nach, seit, von, zu

Accusative or dative: an, auf, hinter, in, neben, über, unter, vor, zwischen

Genitive: außerhalb, statt, trotz, während, wegen

(page 19)

1 **1** c, **2** e, **3** f, **4** a, **5** h, **6** g, **7** b, **8** d

2 **a** Sie kommt gut <u>mit ihren</u> Eltern aus.

b Mein Bruder spart <u>auf ein</u> neues Rad.

c Ich warte schon seit 30 Minuten <u>auf den</u> Bus!

d Interessierst du dich <u>für klassische</u> Musik?

e Was hältst du <u>von unserem</u> neuen Direktor?

f Igitt! Diese Bonbons schmecken <u>nach</u> Fisch!

g Wir freuen uns <u>auf die</u> Sommerferien.

h Ich muss zehn Minuten lang <u>über meine</u> Hobbys sprechen.

i–l open-ended

3 **a** während der Mittagspause, **b** aus dem Haus, **c** unter den Stuhl, **d** bei den Schmidts, **e** von meinem Onkel, **f** die Straße entlang, **g** durch den Park, **h** nach einer Woche, **i** für seine Tante, **j** in die Bäckerei, **k** um die Ecke, **l** für einen Monat, **m** an die Wand, **n** vor das Haus, **o** wegen seines Lehrers/seiner Lehrerin, **p** auf dem Schrank, **q** ohne ihr Geld, **r** hinter die Tür, **s** trotz des Preises, **t** statt eines Geschenks, **u** gegenüber dem Hotel/dem Hotel gegenüber, **v** neben der Kirche, **w** außer den Kindern, **x** außerhalb des Sportzentrums, **y** zwischen die Tische, **z** über das Haus, **aa** mit meinen Großeltern, **ab** zum Supermarkt, **ac** in das/ins Theater, **ad** gegen einen Baum

(page 20)

1 Das <u>südwestafrikanische</u> Namibia ist ein <u>schönes</u> Land, aber es gibt dort <u>große</u> Kontraste. Windhoek, die ziemlich <u>moderne</u> Hauptstadt, hat <u>riesige</u> Wohnblocks, <u>tolle</u> Einkaufszentren, <u>breite</u> Straßen mit <u>lauten</u> Autos. Auf dem Land aber sind viele Menschen sehr <u>arm</u>. Sie wohnen in <u>primitiven</u> Hütten ohne <u>moderne</u> Annehmlichkeiten wie Elektrizität und Wasser. Es gibt viel Wüste, wo das Leben sehr <u>hart</u> ist. Es gibt aber auch eine <u>lange</u> Küste am Atlantik. Dort kann man <u>verschiedene</u> Wassersportarten betreiben. <u>Ausländische</u> Touristen besuchen Namibia, um die <u>imposante</u> Landschaft zu sehen und die <u>schönen</u> <u>afrikanischen</u> Tiere zu fotografieren.

2 open-ended

3 Suggested answer (others are possible): **a** süß, **b** intelligent, **c** müde, **d** alt, bequem, **e** teuer, **f** wunderbar

(page 21)

1 **a** feminine/nominative, **b** masculine/nominative, **c** plural/accusative, **d** neuter/genitive, **e** masculine/dative, **f** feminine/accusative

2 **a** masculine/accusative, **b** feminine/dative, **c** neuter/genitive, **d** feminine/nominative, **e** neuter/accusative, **f** neuter/dative

3 **a** deutsche, **b** neunten, **c** interessanten, **d** anderen, **e** neuen, **f** deutsche

4 **a** Die junge Frau Krohn hat schon vier Kinder.

b Markus ist der einzige Sohn.

c Die anderen Kinder sind alle Mädchen.

d Die Kinder spielen oft mit den stolzen Großeltern.

e Es ist manchmal schwierig in diesem kleinen Haus.

f Für den jungen Vater ist es auch nicht leicht.

(page 22)

1 **a** guter, **b** großes, **c** neuen, **d** normale, **e** jüngeren, **f** anderen, **g** elegante, **h** brauner

2 **a** Meine Familie hat einen neu<u>en</u> Hund.

b Unsere schön<u>en</u> Katzen sind nicht froh darüber!

c Früher hatten wir kein groß<u>es</u> Haus und keine Haustiere.

d Jetzt aber wohnen wir auf einem alt<u>en</u> Bauernhof mit einem groß<u>en</u> Garten.

e Das Haus ist am Rande eines hübsch<u>en</u> Dorfs.

f Es gibt einen klein<u>en</u> Supermarkt und eine langweilige Kneipe.

g Wir haben keine interessant<u>en</u> Vereine.

h Manchmal fahre ich mit einer freundlich<u>en</u> Nachbarin in die Stadt.

3 **A:** Katrin gibt eine <u>große</u> Party und ich brauche einen <u>neuen</u> Rock.

L: Ja, sie lädt die <u>ganze</u> Klasse ein und ich gehe auch mit meinem <u>neuen</u> Freund hin.

A: Der ist so <u>süß</u>. Was trägst du zu dieser <u>tollen</u> Party?

L: Ich trage meine <u>neue</u> Jeans, aber ich möchte ein <u>neues</u> T-Shirt.

A: Siehst du das <u>grüne</u> T-Shirt dort drüben?

L: Schick – ich habe kein <u>gutes</u> T-Shirt. Und du, siehst du diesen <u>blauen</u> Rock?

A: Der Rock ist <u>schön</u>, aber die <u>hässliche</u> Farbe gefällt mir nicht. Und der Preis dieses <u>schwarzen</u> Rockes ist viel zu <u>hoch</u>.

L: Gehen wir in ein <u>anderes</u> Geschäft. Welche <u>modernen</u> Modegeschäfte gibt es hier?

A: Es gibt die <u>großen</u> Kaufhäuser. Sie haben bestimmt einen <u>billigen</u> Rock für mich.

L: Also, wir gehen in einen <u>billigen</u> Laden und kaufen uns die <u>perfekte</u> Kleidung für eine <u>wichtige</u> Party!

(page 23)

1
  a Ich höre sehr gern <u>kreative Musik</u>. − f, sing., A

  b <u>Laute Musik</u> kann gefährlich sein. − f, sing., N

  c <u>Mit guten Noten</u> hat man kaum <u>große Probleme</u>. − f, pl., D, / n, pl., A

  d Es soll gesund sein, <u>in kaltem Wasser</u> zu baden. − n, sing., D

  e Ich habe <u>zwei süße Katzen</u>. − f, pl., A

  f Das Mittelmeer hat <u>viele goldene Strände</u>. − m, pl., A

  g Die Farbe <u>einiger neuer Autos</u> finde ich furchtbar. − n, pl., G

  h Meine Schwester bekommt <u>tolle Geschenke</u>. − n, pl., A

2 **a** deutsche, **b** englische, **c** *Gute, schlechte,* **d** schwarzen, grünen, **e** Frisches, warmes, **f** guten, schöne, **g** interessanten, **h** heißes, teure

3

der/dieser/jener/jeder/welcher			
-e	-e	-e	-en
-en	-e	-e	-en
-en	-en	-en	-en
-en	-en	-en	-en

ein/kein/mein/dein/sein/ihr/unser/euer			
-er	-e	-es	-en
-en	-e	-es	-en
-en	-en	-en	-en
-en	-en	-en	-en

No determiner			
-er	-e	-es	-e
-en	-e	-es	-e
-en	-er	-en	-er
-em	-er	-em	-en

(page 24)

1 **1** e, **2** i, **3** b, **4** k, **5** g, **6** j, **7** a, **8** l, **9** h, **10** c, **11** f, **12** d

2 **a** etwas Blaues, **b** mit viel Gutem, **c** nichts Wichtiges, **d** wenig Besonderes/Spezielles, **e** auf etwas Kaltem, **f** nichts Heißes

3 open-ended

4 **a** Er wünschte mir alles <u>Gute</u>.

  b Sie haben uns alles <u>Mögliche</u> angeboten.

  c Sie hat alles <u>Schmutzige</u> in die Waschmaschine gesteckt.

  d Wir haben alles <u>Gesunde</u> gegessen.

(page 25)

1

Adjective	Meaning	Comparative	Meaning
schön	*beautiful*	schöner	*more beautiful*
<u>alt</u>	*<u>old</u>*	älter	*older*
<u>jung</u>	*<u>young</u>*	jünger	*<u>younger</u>*
kalt	*cold*	<u>kälter</u>	*<u>colder</u>*
arm	*poor*	ärmer	*poorer*
warm	*warm*	wärmer	*<u>warmer</u>*
lang	*long*	länger	*<u>longer</u>*
intelligent	*intelligent*	intelligenter	*more intelligent*
wichtig	*important*	wichtiger	*more important*
<u>faul</u>	*lazy*	fauler	*lazier*
aktiv	*active*	aktiver	*more active*
durstig	*thirsty*	<u>durstiger</u>	*thirstier*
hungrig	*hungry*	hungriger	*hungrier*
billig	*cheap*	<u>billiger</u>	*cheaper*
teuer	*dear/ expensive*	teurer	*dearer/more expensive*
<u>gesund</u>	*healthy*	gesünder	*healthier*
gefährlich	*dangerous*	gefährlicher	*more dangerous*
hoch	*high*	höher	*higher*
gut	*good*	besser	*better*
+ 4 more adjectives of own choice			

2 **a** Diese Straße ist <u>länger</u>.

  b In den Geschäften hat man eine <u>bessere</u> Auswahl.

  c Dieser Wohnblock ist <u>höher</u>.

  d Ein <u>älterer</u> Mann wohnt im zehnten Stock.

  e Das Geschenk ist für ein <u>freundlicheres</u> Mädchen.

  f Frau Bolle will mit <u>jüngeren</u> Leuten arbeiten.

3 **a** Viele Leute treiben Sport, um <u>fitter</u> zu werden.

  b Sport spielt heute eine <u>wichtigere</u> Rolle im Leben vieler Deutschen als vor 20 Jahren.

  c Es gibt auch <u>interessantere</u> Sportarten als früher.

  d In einer <u>größeren</u> Sporthalle sieht man viele Sportarten auf einmal.

  e Weniger Deutsche als Engländer spielen Golf, vielleicht weil es in Deutschland <u>teurer</u> ist.

(page 26)

4 **a** Schokolade ist nicht so gesund wie Obst.

b Markus ist genauso schlank wie Andreas.

c Anja ist fauler als Eva.

d Ich bin jünger als mein Bruder.

e Meine Mutter ist nicht so alt wie mein Vater.

f Bücher sind besser als Filme.

g Das T-Shirt ist genauso teuer wie das Hemd.

h Der Frühling ist nicht so kalt wie der Winter

i Süßigkeiten sind schlechter als Hamburger.

1 **a** our best teacher

b the cheapest shop

c the most beautiful colours

d in the most interesting film

e for his eldest/oldest child

2 **a** teuerste, **b** fleißigsten, **c** schlechteste, **d** ärmsten, **e** beste

3 **a** die ärmsten Leute/Menschen

b im (in dem) längsten Film

c nach der schlimmsten/schlechtesten Prüfung

d die nächste Stadt

e Peter ist mein ältester Cousin.

(page 27)

1 **a** Monika lernt für die Prüfungen, aber sie macht <u>regelmäßig</u> Pausen. (regularly)

b Sie lernt <u>besser</u>, wenn sie Musik hört. (better)

c Ihre Brüder essen <u>immer gesund</u>. (always, healthily)

d <u>Abends</u> kann ich mich <u>nicht so gut</u> konzentrieren. (in the evening(s), not so well)

e <u>Auf der Autobahn</u> fährt man <u>oft</u> zu <u>schnell</u>. (on the motorway, often, too fast)

f Ich will nicht arbeiten – ich möchte <u>in Ruhe</u> lesen. (quietly/in peace)

g Ich werde mich <u>warm</u> anziehen, weil es kalt ist. (warm(ly)

h Wir warten <u>nervös</u> auf den Direktor. (nervously)

2 The ending –<u>ly</u> in English is often used for adverbs.

3 **a** Waschmittel A wäscht alles sauber, B wäscht alles <u>sauberer</u>, aber C wäscht alles am <u>saubersten</u>. – Washing powder A washes everything clean(ly), B washes everything cleaner / more cleanly, but C washes (the) cleanest / most cleanly.

b Mein Vater fährt <u>vorsichtig</u>, aber meine Mutter fährt vorsichtiger und meine Oma fährt <u>am vorsichtigsten</u>.

– My father drives carefully, but my mother drives more carefully and my grandmother drives (the) most carefully (of all).

c Ich schwimme <u>viel</u>, ich jogge mehr und <u>am meisten</u> fahre ich Rad. – I swim a lot, I jog more and most of all I cycle.

d Bananen schmecken <u>gut</u>, Orangen schmecken <u>besser</u>, aber Äpfel schmecken am besten. – Bananas taste good, oranges taste better, but apples taste best (of all).

e (open-ended)

4 **a** am lautesten, **b** am pünktlichsten, **c** am höchsten, **d** am längsten

(page 28)

1 **Food: 1** *Schokolade* / chocolate, **2** *Kekse* / biscuits, **3** *Obst* / fruit

Sport: 1 *Schwimmen* / swimming, **2** *Leichtathletik* / athletics, **3** *Tennis* / playing tennis

Other activities: 1 *Fernsehen* / watching TV, **2** *Lesen* / reading, **3** *Geige* / playing the violin

2 **a** Ich esse gern Brot.

b Er spielt lieber Fußball.

c Am liebsten hört sie Musik.

d Wir lernen gern Deutsch.

e Sie sehen nicht gern fern.

f Trinkst du/Trinken Sie lieber Tee oder Kaffee?

3 **1** b, **2** e, **3** a, **4** f, **5** c, **6** d

(page 29)

1

wann	<u>when</u>
wie	how
wo	<u>where</u>
warum	why
wie viel(e)...	how much (how <u>many</u>) ...
was	<u>what</u>
<u>*wer*</u> *(wen, wem)*	who (whom)
was <u>für</u>...	what <u>sort</u> of ...

2 **a** wann, **b** was, **c** was für, **d** wie viel, **e** wo, **f** warum

3 (suggested questions; others are possible)

a Wann fährst du (fahren Sie) nach Hause?

b Warum liest du (lesen Sie) dieses Buch?

c Wie viele Briefmarken hast du (haben Sie)?

d Was macht (spielt) Thomas?

e Wo spielt er Fußball?

f Wie fährst/kommst du/fahren Sie zur Schule?

4 Open-ended.

(page 30)

1 **(Time)**

manchmal	<u>sometimes</u>
immer	always
o<u>f</u>t	often
nie	never
ab und zu	now and again
dann und wann	now and then
so bald wie möglich	as <u>soon</u> as possible
nächste Woche	next <u>week</u>
nächstes Wochenende	next <u>weekend</u>
nächsten <u>Montag</u>	next Monday
letztes Jahr	last year
letzte <u>Woche</u>	last week
letzten <u>Dienstag</u>	last Tuesday
nach der Schule	after <u>school</u>
vor dem Frühstück	<u>before</u> breakfast
vor drei Jahren	<u>three</u> years ago
vor zwei Monaten	two <u>months</u> ago
jeden <u>Tag</u>	every day
sonntags	every <u>Sunday</u>, on Sundays
um 8 Uhr	at 8 o'clock
im Sommer	in the <u>summer</u>

(Manner)

mit dem Bus	by bus
mit Freunden	with <u>friends</u>
mit meiner <u>Familie</u>	with my family

(Place)

hier	<u>here</u>
dort	there
in der Stadt	in town
in die Stadt	into <u>town</u>
nach Berlin	to Berlin
zum Supermarkt	<u>to</u> the supermarket

2 **a** letztes Wochenende
b montags/jeden Montag
c vor einem Monat
d nächstes Jahr
e nach Freiburg
f mit einem Freund/mit einer Freundin

3 **a** Ich fahre morgen mit der Klasse nach München.
b Man kann sonntags mit dem Hund am Fluss spazieren gehen.
c Viele junge Deutsche verbringen ein Jahr als Au-Pair in England.

(page 31)

1

ein bisschen	a <u>bit</u>
ein wenig	a little
einfach	simply
ganz	quite, completely
gar nicht	<u>not</u> at all
kaum	hardly
sehr	<u>very</u>
so	so
total	totally
überhaupt <u>nicht</u>	not at all
viel (+ comparative)	much more ...
ziemlich	<u>quite/pretty/rather</u>, fairly
zu	too

2 open-ended
3 **1** verb, **2** one, **3** phrase, **4** adjective, **5** endings, **6** superlative, **7** question, **8** time, **9** emphasis
4 open-ended

(page 32)

1 **a** *<u>mich</u>* – accusative, with preposition *für*
b *<u>Wir</u>* – nominative, subject of the verb (can)
   sie – accusative, direct object of the verb (do)
c *ich* – nominative, subject of the verbs (love, spend)
   ihr – dative, with preposition *bei*
d *ihr* – nominative, subject of the verb (want)
   Er – nominative, subject of the verb (is)
e *Sie* – nominative, subject of the verb (are going)
   mir – dative, with preposition *mit*
f *Sie* – nominative, subject of the verb (have set off)
   <u>mich</u> – accusative, with preposition *ohne*

2 **a** Kannst du <u>mich</u> hören?
b Ich kann <u>dich</u> nicht sehen.
c Gib <u>mir</u> deine Hand.
d Soll ich <u>dir</u> die Butter reichen?
e Was möchtest <u>du</u> als Nachtisch?

3 **a** Laura und Leon sind Kinder – <u>sie</u> sprechen mit ihrem Vater:
b Vati, gib <u>uns</u> bitte 5 Euro.

c Ich habe <u>euch</u> schon gesagt – nein!

d Aber <u>wir</u> wollen einen Comic kaufen.

e <u>Ihr</u> lest zu viele blöde Comics.

f Ja, aber <u>sie</u> sind lustig.

(page 33)

1 **a** Ich verstehe mich gut mit <u>ihr</u>.

b Ich sehe <u>ihn</u> jeden Tag.

c Das ist mein Buch. <u>Es</u> ist sehr interessant.

d Wo ist meine Jacke? Ich finde <u>sie</u> nicht.

e Der Zug hat Verspätung. <u>Er</u> kommt in 10 Minuten an.

f Ich habe meinen Kuli verloren. Hast du <u>ihn</u> gesehen?

2 **a** Wir helfen <u>ihnen</u> bei der Arbeit.

b Diese Schuhe gefallen <u>ihr</u> sehr.

c Warte mal, Erika, ich sage <u>dir</u> die Antwort.

d Unsere Schuluniform gefällt <u>uns</u> überhaupt nicht.

e Ich habe <u>ihm</u> meine Hausaufgaben gegeben.

f Nein, Mutti, deine Jacke passt <u>mir</u> überhaupt nicht.

g Herr Krohn, ich möchte <u>Ihnen</u> meine Arbeit zeigen.

h Also, Kinder, ich erzähle <u>euch</u> eine tolle Geschichte.

3 **a** Was ist mit <u>dir</u> los?

b Otto hat einen neue Freundin. <u>Sie</u> ist nicht sehr nett.

c <u>Er</u> hat <u>ihr</u> eine Halskette gegeben.

d Hast <u>du</u> etwas für <u>mich</u>?

e Kannst du <u>mir</u> einen Witz erzählen?

f Bastian? Ich finde <u>ihn</u> sehr sympathisch.

g Wie war die Sendung? Ich habe <u>sie</u> nicht gesehen.

h Frau Herbert, ich möchte mit <u>Ihnen</u> sprechen.

i Da fährt der Bus – ich habe <u>ihn</u> verpasst.

j Meine Oma wohnt zur Zeit bei <u>uns</u>.

(page 34)

1 **a** Ich dusche <u>mich</u> jeden Morgen.

b Für die Sportstunde ziehen wir <u>uns</u> natürlich um.

c Thomas und Martin fühlen <u>sich</u> nicht wohl.

d Thomas legt <u>sich</u> auf sein Bett.

e Interessieren Sie <u>sich</u> für Volleyball?

f Meine Schwester zieht <u>sich</u> immer vor dem Frühstück an.

g Mein Kaninchen freut <u>sich</u> auf den Salat!

h Das ist besser – ich habe <u>mich</u> schön ausgeruht.

i Ihr wascht <u>euch</u> am besten im Badezimmer, nicht in der Küche.

2 (direct objects underlined, **reflexive pronouns bold**)

a Alexander wäscht **sich** <u>die Hände</u> vor dem Essen. – Alexander washes his hands before eating.

b Kaufst du **dir** <u>eine neue Jeans</u> in der Stadt? – Are you buying yourself a new pair of jeans in town?

c Heute Abend sehe ich **mir** <u>einen alten Film</u> an. – This evening I'm going to watch an old film.

d Zum Geburtstag wünschst sie **sich** <u>ein Mountainbike</u>. – For her birthday she wants a mountain bike.

e Hast du **dir** <u>die Zähne</u> geputzt? – Have you cleaned your teeth?

f Kämm **dir** bitte <u>die Haare</u>! – Please comb your hair!

3 **a** Meine Familie interessiert <u>sich</u> für Sport.

b Ich habe <u>mir</u> einen Hamburger gekauft.

c Fühlst du <u>dich</u> jetzt krank?

d Wir haben <u>uns</u> nach dem Spiel geduscht.

e Habt ihr <u>euch</u> das Spiel im Fernsehen angesehen?

f Was wünschen Sie <u>sich</u> zu Weihnachten?

(page 35)

1 **a** Niemand, **b** jemanden, **c** jemandem, **d** niemandem, **e** Jemand

2 **a** wen, **b** Wer, **c** Wem, **d** Wen, **e** Wer, **f** wem

3 **1** c, **2** f, **3** a, **4** h, **5** e, **6** d, **7** b, **8** g

4

<u>der</u>	die	<u>das</u>	die
<u>den</u>	die	das	<u>die</u>
<u>dem</u>	der	dem	denen

(page 36)

5 **a** Basketball, der ein Sport für junge Leute ist, gefällt mir sehr.

b Meine beste Lehrerin, die Frau Ohm heißt, unterrichtet Physik.

c Das blaue Rad, das vorne im Sportgeschäft steht, kostet €1000.

d Die Olympischen Spiele, die alle vier Jahre stattfinden, sind sehr interessant.

6 **a** N, **b** D, **c** A, **d** A, **e** N, **f** A

7 **a** 5 – The young people (that) I spoke to are studying foreign languages.

b 4 – The lady who gave me €20 was very nice.

c 2 – The girl who sits next to me is very good at German.

d 1 – The computer we played on yesterday is broken now.

8 **a** die, **b** dem, **c** das, **d** denen, **e** die, **f** der

(page 37)

1 **a** Ich <u>verbringe</u> ziemlich viel Zeit im Internet.

b − Wann <u>beginnt</u> der Film?
− Die erste Vorstellung <u>ist</u> um 19 Uhr.

c Ich <u>möchte</u> zwei Karten für morgen Abend <u>reservieren</u>.

d Ich <u>habe</u> dieses Handy letzte Woche <u>gekauft,</u> aber es <u>funktioniert</u> nicht.

e Ich <u>bin</u> auf den Weihnachtsmarkt <u>gegangen</u> und <u>habe</u> meine Geschenke <u>gekauft</u>.

f Letztes Jahr <u>haben</u> wir viel <u>gegessen</u> und <u>getrunken</u> und <u>getanzt</u>.

g Ich <u>werde</u> nächstes Jahr zum Musikfest in Nürnberg <u>fahren</u>.

2 Young Germans speak and <u>write</u> to each other using the informal (<u>familiar</u>) forms:

du (<u>one</u> person)

ihr (more than one <u>person</u>).

<u>Family</u> members also usually call each other *du*.

The possessive pronouns for informal '<u>your</u>' are *dein/deine/dein; euer/eure/euer.*

The <u>reflexive</u> forms are: *dich* (accusative), *dir* (<u>dative</u>); *euch* (both <u>accusative</u> and dative).

When speaking or writing to someone <u>older</u> or not well known to you or in a position of <u>authority</u>, use the <u>formal</u> (polite) *Sie* form. This is the <u>same</u> for one and for more than one person.

The <u>possessive</u> pronoun for formal 'your' is *'Ihr'* for both singular and plural.

The reflexive form for the formal *Sie* is <u>always</u> *sich*.

3

Inf. sing.	Inf. pl.	Form. sing./pl.
du	ihr	Sie
dich	euch	Sie
dir	euch	Ihnen
dein/deine/dein	euer/eure/euer	Ihr/Ihre/Ihr
dich	euch	sich

(page 38)

1 **a** Gehst du am Wochenende zur Party?

b Wann haben Sie diesen Film gesehen?

c Wie bist du zur Schule gekommen?

d Bleibt Frau Müller heute zu Hause?

e Warum hat er sich nicht gewaschen?

f Wo haben die Kinder ihren Ball verloren?

2 **a** P, **b** N, **c** N, **d** N, **e** P, **f** N

3 **a** Ich kenne diesen Jungen nicht.

b Wir haben dieses Buch nicht gelesen.

c Meine Mutter hat keinen Wagen.

d Also kann ich nicht mit ihr fahren. / Also kann ich mit ihr nicht fahren.

e Unsere Sporthalle ist nicht sehr modern.

f Ich esse dein Stück Kuchen nicht.

g Wir möchten keine Party zum Geburtstag haben.

h Ich darf die Ohrringe nicht kaufen/keine Ohrringe kaufen, weil ich kein/nicht viel Geld habe.

(page 39)

1 (<u>modal verbs underlined</u>, **infinitives bold**)

a Wir <u>wollen</u> am Wochenende Handball **spielen**. − We want to play handball at the weekend.

b Wann <u>kannst</u> du mir ein Computerspiel **kaufen**? − When can you buy me a computer game?

c Ich <u>darf</u> im Sommer nach Spanien **fahren**. − I'm allowed to (I can) go to Spain in the summer.

d Heute <u>soll</u> ich **lernen**, aber ich <u>will</u> nicht. − Today I'm supposed to study (be studying), but I don't want to.

e Meine Eltern <u>mögen</u> es nicht, wenn ich spät nach Hause komme. − My parents don't like it when I come home late.

f Ich <u>mag</u> nicht **tanzen**, weil ich nicht gut **tanzen** <u>kann</u>. − I don't like dancing because I can't dance well.

g Wann <u>musst</u> du nach Hause **gehen**? − When do you have to (must you) go home?

h <u>Können</u> Sie diese Flaschen bitte zum Recycling **bringen**? − Please can you take these bottles to the bottle bank/recycling container?

2 **1** c, **2** f, **3** a, **4** e, **5** b, **6** d

3 open-ended

(page 40)

4

dürfen	können	mögen
to be allowed to	*to be able to (can)*	*to like (to)*
darf	kann	mag
darfst	kannst	magst
darf	kann	mag
dürfen	können	mögen
dürft	könnt	mögt
dürfen	können	mögen
dürfen	können	mögen

müssen	sollen	wollen
to have to (must)	*to be supposed to*	*to want to*
muss	soll	will
musst	sollst	willst
muss	soll	will
müssen	sollen	wollen
müsst	sollt	wollt
müssen	sollen	wollen
müssen	sollen	wollen

5 **a** Ich soll heute in die Stadt (fahren/gehen).

b Ich darf nicht ins Kino (gehen).

c Sie wollen fernsehen.

d Kannst du Französisch (sprechen)?

e Die Lehrer müssen jeden Abend arbeiten.

1 **1** e, **2** i, **3** b, **4** k, **5** h, **6** a, **7** l, **8** j, **9** c, **10** f, **11** d, **12** g

(page 41)

1 open-ended

2 **a** Der Zug kommt um 14 Uhr in Köln an. – The train arrives in (gets into) Cologne at 14.00 (2 pm).

b Ich wache immer vor meiner Schwester auf. – I always wake up before my sister.

c Samstags kaufe ich mit meinen Freunden in der Stadt ein. – On Saturdays I go shopping in town with my friends.

d Mein Brieffreund packt seinen Koffer aus. – My penfriend is unpacking his case.

e Am Sonntag bereitet mein Vater das Mittagessen vor. – On Sunday my father is preparing lunch.

(page 42)

3 open-ended

4 **a** S, **b** I, **c** I, **d** S, **e** I, **f** I, **g** S, **h** S

5 **a** Normalerweise stehen wir um Viertel vor sieben auf.

b Meine Mutter bereitet unser Frühstück (uns das Frühstück) vor.

c Ich verlasse das Haus um halb acht.

d Der Bus kommt ziemlich schnell an der Schule an.

e Ich bespreche meine Hausaufgaben mit meinen Freunden.

f Wir verstehen uns gut mit den Lehrern.

(page 43)

1

ich	mich	mir
du	dich	dir
er, sie, es	sich	sich
wir	uns	uns
ihr	euch	euch
Sie	sich	sich
sie	sich	sich

2
sich anziehen	to get dressed
sich ausziehen	to get undressed
sich umziehen	to get changed
sich ausruhen	to have a rest
sich duschen	to have a shower
sich erinnern (an etwas)	to remember (something)
sich freuen (auf etwas)	to look forward (to something)
sich fühlen	to feel
sich hinlegen	to lie down
sich hinsetzen	to sit down
sich interessieren (für etwas)	to be interested (in something)
sich sonnen	to sunbathe

3 **1** d, **2** h, **3** b, **4** i, **5** g, **6** a, **7** e, **8** c, **9** f

4 open-ended

(page 44)

5 open-ended

6 **a** D, **b** D, **c** A, **d** D, **e** D, **f** A, **g** A

7 **a** Ich wasche mir die Hände vor dem Mittagessen.

b Er kauft sich einen neuen Computer.

c Wir können uns einen Kuchen leisten. / Wir leisten uns einen Kuchen.

d Hast du dir die Zähne geputzt?

e Sie zieht sich einen Pullover an.

f Ich mache mir Sorgen um meinen Freund/meine Freundin.

(page 45)

1 **1** c, **2** d, **3** a, **4** e, **5** a, **6** f, **7** d, **8** b, **9** c, **10** d

2 **a** ich wohne, **b** du arbeitest, **c** er stellt, **d** sie bürstet sich, **e** es braucht, **f** man macht, **g** wir hassen, **h** ihr mietet, **i** Sie kaufen ein, **j** sie sagen

(page 46)

3 **1** sieht, **2** gibt, **3** weiß, **4** hilft, **5** schläft, **6** läuft , **7** trifft, **8** fahrt, **9** nimmt, **10** verlässt, **11** fährt, **12** Seht

4 **1** sprechen, spreche, sprichst, spricht, sprecht, sprechen

2 helfen, helfe, hilfst, hilft, helft, helfen

3 essen, esse, isst, isst, esst, essen

4 halten, halte, hältst, hält, haltet, halten

5 lassen, lasse, lässt, lässt, lasst, lassen

6 nehmen, nehme, nimmst, nimmt, nehmt, nehmen

7 fahren, fahre, fährst, fährt, fahrt, fahren

8 sich waschen, wasche mich, wäschst dich, wäscht sich, wascht euch, waschen sich

9 fallen, falle, fällst, fällt, fallt, fallen

10 einschlafen, schlafe ein, schläfst ein, schläft ein, schlaft ein, schlafen ein

5 **a** Normalerweise <u>nimmt</u> Wolfgang den Bus, aber heute <u>fährt</u> er mit dem Rad zur Schule. – Normally Wolfgang takes the bus, but today he's cycling to school.

b <u>Esst</u> ihr jeden Tag etwas in der Pause? – Do you eat something at break every day?

c Ich <u>wasche</u> mir immer das Gesicht nach dem Essen. – I always wash my face after eating

d Warum <u>läufst</u> du weg? Es <u>gibt</u> noch viel zu sehen. – Why are you running away? There's still a lot to see.

(page 47)

6 **a** irregular, **b** *du*, **c** perfect, **d** auxiliary, **e** *haben*, **f** *habt*

7

	haben	*to have*
ich	<u>habe</u>	*I have*
du	hast	*you have*
er/sie/es	<u>hat</u>	*he/she/it has*
wir	haben	*we have*
ihr	habt	*you have*
Sie	<u>haben</u>	*you have*
sie	haben	*they have*

8 **1** to be, **2** irregular, **3** tense, **4** *ist*, **5** have

9

	sein	*to be*
ich	<u>bin</u>	*I am*
du	bist	*you are*
er/sie/es	<u>ist</u>	*he/she/it is*
wir	sind	*we are*
ihr	seid	*you are*
Sie	sind	*you are*
sie	<u>sind</u>	*they are*

10 **1** to become, **2** jobs, **3** *du*, **4** future, **5** am going

11

	werden	*to become (etc.)*
ich	<u>werde</u>	*I become*
du	wirst	*you become*
er/sie/es	wird	*he/she/it becomes*
wir	<u>werden</u>	*we become*
ihr	<u>werdet</u>	*you become*
Sie	<u>werden</u>	*you become*
sie	<u>werden</u>	*they become*

12 **a** Hast, **b** sind, **c** wirst, **d** hat, **e** seid, **f** wird

(page 48)

1 **a** 1, **b** 3, **c** 4, **d** 2, **e** 6, **f** 5, **g** 2, **h** 1, **i** 6, **j** 3, **k** 2, **l** 5, **m** 4, **n** 3, **o** 1

2 (<u>auxiliaries underlined</u>, **past participles bold**)

a Was <u>hast</u> du gestern **gemacht**? – What did you do yesterday?

b Ich <u>bin</u> mit Max in die Stadt **gefahren**. – I went into town with Max.

c Wir <u>haben</u> neue Kleidung **gekauft**. – We bought (some) new clothes.

d Nach dem Abendessen <u>habe</u> ich Karten **gespielt**. – After dinner/supper I played cards.

e Wann <u>bist</u> du ins Bett **gegangen**? – When did you go to bed?

f Gegen 11 Uhr <u>ist</u> meine Mutter ins Zimmer **gekommen**. – At about 11 o'clock my mother came into my/the room.

g Sie <u>hat</u> „Gute Nacht" **gesagt**. – She said good night.

h Aber dann <u>habe</u> ich das Buch **gelesen**, das du mir **gegeben** <u>hast</u>. – But then I read the book (that) you gave me.

i Dieses Buch <u>habe</u> ich sehr interessant **gefunden**. – I found this book very interesting.

j Heute Morgen <u>habe</u> ich lange **geschlafen**. – This morning I slept for a long time.

(page 49)

3 **a** getanzt, **b** gespart, **c** gereicht, **d** gemacht, **e** gearbeitet, **f** gemietet, **g** gelernt, **h** gehört, **i** gelebt

4 open-ended

5 **a** hat ... genommen, **b** habe ... geholfen, **c** ist ... geblieben, **d** hat ... gegessen, **e** hat ... begonnen, **f** hast ... gehalten, **g** haben ... gebrochen, **h** seid ... gewesen, **i** sind ... gefahren, **j** haben ... geschlossen, **k** bin ... gegangen, **l** hast ... geschrieben, **m** hat gestanden, **n** habt ... getroffen, **o** ist ... geworden, **p** haben ... gesprochen

(page 50)

6 **a** bringen – to bring, **b** denken – to think, **c** haben – to have, **d** kennen – to know (people, places), **e** senden – to send, **f** wissen – to know (facts)

7 **a** aufgeräumt, **b** ferngesehen, **c** eingeschlafen, **d** aufgewacht, **e** angezogen, **f** ausgefüllt, **g** mitgekommen, **h** mitgebracht

8 **a** erhalten, **b** diskutiert, **c** verstanden, **d** begrüßt, **e** fotografiert, **f** telefoniert, **g** versucht, **h** probiert

(page 51)

9 **a** sein, gehen, **b** haben, haben, **c** sein, werden, **d** haben, sehen, **e** haben, bekommen, **f** sein, bleiben, **g** sein, aufstehen, **h** haben, einladen

10 **a** sind, **b** hat, **c** habe, **d** Seid, **e** haben, **f** ist

11 (allow different word order if correct)

    a Ihr habt euch jeden Tag in Spanien gesonnt.

    b Wir haben uns für das Konzert angezogen.

    c Hast du dich als Kind für Plüschtiere interessiert?

    d Ich habe mir heute ein neues Hemd gekauft.

    e Nach dem Spiel haben sie sich hingesetzt.

(page 52)

12 **1** past, **2** auxiliary, **3** past participle, **4** *haben*, **5** reflexive, **6** *sein*, **7** place, **8** –ge–, **9** –t, **10** –en, **11** stem, **12** Modal, **13** middle, **14** do not

13 **a** ich habe mich gewaschen, **b** du hast gesagt, **c** er hat gemusst, **d** sie ist angekommen, **e** es ist gewesen, **f** wir haben gefunden, **g** ihr habt geliebt, **h** Sie sind geschwommen, **i** du hast dich befunden, **j** ich habe verwendet

14 **a** Wir <u>haben</u> Interviews in der Klasse <u>gemacht</u>.

    b Es <u>hat</u> mir Leid <u>getan</u>!

    c Ich <u>bin</u> nach Paris <u>geflogen</u>.

    d Du <u>hast</u> gute Noten <u>gekriegt</u>.

    e Herbert <u>hat</u> in der Schule später als ich <u>angefangen</u>.

    f Elke <u>hat</u> manchmal im Café <u>gegessen</u>.

    g Die Deutschstunde <u>ist</u> zu kurz <u>gewesen</u>.

    h Ich <u>habe</u> Fremdsprachen <u>gewählt</u>.

    i Du <u>hast</u> dir deine Wahlfächer <u>überlegt</u>.

    j Sie <u>ist</u> Ingenieurin <u>geworden</u>.

15 open-ended

(page 53)

1 **a** er telefonierte, **b** sie sagte, **c** es machte, **d** ich kaufte ein, **e** du antwortetest, **f** man lernte, **g** ihr setztet euch, **h** Sie studierten, **i** wir sparten, **j** sie kriegten

2 **1** e, **2** h, **3** a, **4** f, **5** l, **6** b, **7** g, **8** j, **9** c, **10** k, **11** i, **12** d

3 open-ended   **4** open-ended

(page 54)

5 **1** changes, **2** stem, **3** present, **4** weak, **5** *ich*, **6** same, **7** *er/sie/es*, **8** exactly

(page 55)

1 **a** ... vorher <u>hatte</u> sie an der Unit <u>studiert</u>.

    b Er <u>hatte</u> seine Kreditkarte <u>verloren</u> ...

    c Max <u>hatte</u> nicht <u>gemerkt</u>, dass der Bus schon <u>angekommen war</u>.

    d Wir <u>waren</u> so schnell <u>gefahren</u>, ...

    e ... davor <u>hatte</u> ich meistens *Rammstein* <u>gehört</u>.

    f ..., weil sie vor dem Spiel lange <u>trainiert hatten</u>.

    g Früher <u>war</u> ich nie in ein Konzert <u>gegangen</u>, ...

    h ... das <u>hatte</u> ich nicht <u>erwartet</u>!

    i ..., aber ich <u>hatte</u> den Film schon <u>gesehen</u>.

    j ..., weil sie das Wasser nicht <u>getrunken hatten</u>.

2 **a** ich hatte getrunken, **b** wir hatten gespielt, **c** sie hatten sich gewaschen, **d** du hattest verloren, **e** es hatte geregnet, **f** sie war gegangen, **g** ich war geblieben, **h** er war eingestiegen, **i** es war gewesen, **j** Sie waren gefallen

3 **a** hatte, gesagt, **b** waren, angekommen, **c** war, gegangen, **d** hatten, gegessen, **e** hattest, gemacht, **f** warst, gestiegen

(page 56)

1

ich	<u>werde</u>
du	wirst
er/sie/es	<u>wird</u>
wir	werden
ihr	<u>werdet</u>
Sie	werden
sie	<u>werden</u>

2 **a** Hoffentlich <u>werde</u> ich gute Noten <u>bekommen</u>. – I hope I will get good marks.

    b <u>Wirst</u> du nächstes Jahr mit mir Deutsch <u>studieren</u>? – Will you study German with me next year?

    c In den Sommerferien <u>wird</u> mein Freund ein Praktikum bei VW <u>machen</u>. – In the summer holidays my friend is going to / will do work experience with VW.

    d Ihr <u>werdet</u> wie immer mit dem Wohnwagen nach Frankreich <u>fahren</u>. – As always, you will go / be going to France with the caravan.

    e Wenn das Wetter so schlecht bleibt, <u>werden</u> wir nach Hause gehen <u>müssen</u>. – If the weather remains/stays so bad, we will have to go home.

3 open-ended

4 (variations in word order are possible)

   a Nächste Woche fahre ich nach Frankreich. Nächste Woche werde ich nach Frankreich fahren.

   b In den Sommerferien bleiben wir in Schottland. In den Sommerferien werden wir in Schottland bleiben.

   c Nach der Deutschstunde hast du Mathe. Nach der Deutschstunde wirst du Mathe haben.

   d Sie trinkt ein Glas Wasser nach dem Mittagessen. Sie wird nach dem Mittagessen ein Glas Wasser trinken.

   e Nächsten Monat machen sie (macht man) ein Praktikum. Nächsten Monat werden sie (wird man) ein Praktikum machen.

(page 57)

1 a Mein Großvater <u>würde</u> nie ins Ausland <u>fahren</u>. – My grandfather would never go abroad.

   b Wir <u>würden</u> den ganzen Abend am Computer <u>verbringen</u>. – We would spend the whole evening on the computer.

   c Ich <u>würde</u> nicht in einem Büro <u>arbeiten</u>. – I wouldn't work in an office.

   d Zu viele Hausaufgaben <u>würden</u> Schüler müde <u>machen</u>. – Too much homework would make students tired.

   e Ihr <u>würdet</u> keine Zeit für Hobbys <u>haben</u>. – You would have no time for hobbies.

   f <u>Würdest</u> du im Winter nach Spanien <u>fahren</u>? – Would you go to Spain in winter?

   g Wer <u>würde</u> 1000 Euro für ein Kleid <u>ausgeben</u>? – Who would pay 1000 euros for a dress?

   h Nach einem Jahr <u>würden</u> Sie uns <u>vergessen</u>. – After a year you would forget us.

2 a er würde gewinnen, b ihr würdet aufstehen, c wir würden uns duschen, d es würde kosten, e du würdest telefonieren

3 1 c, 2 e, 3 b, 4 d, 5 a

(page 58)

1 a Du <u>musst</u> heute eine Arbeit <u>schreiben</u>.

   b Was <u>werden</u> wir nächste Woche <u>machen/tun</u>?

   c Ich <u>würde</u> mir einen neuen Computer <u>kaufen</u>.

   d <u>Könnt</u> ihr uns nach der Schule <u>telefonieren/anrufen</u>?

   e Im Winter <u>würde</u> sie in die Schweiz <u>fahren/gehen/reisen</u>.

2 a zu studieren, b aufzustehen, c zu verbringen, d zu regnen, e zu essen

3 1 d, 2 a, 3 f, 4 e, 5 c, 6 b

4 a Er wollte viel Geld <u>verdienen</u>, um eine Weltreise <u>zu machen</u>.

   b Du sollst das <u>sagen</u>, ohne den Mund <u>zu bewegen</u>.

   c Sie darf zum Stadion <u>gehen</u>, um ihre Lieblingsmannschaft <u>zu sehen</u>.

   d Wann hoffen Sie, Ihren Führerschein <u>zu machen</u>?

   e Ohne Deutsch <u>zu sprechen</u>, kann man nicht alles <u>verstehen</u>.

   f Wir haben vergessen, einen Pullover <u>mitzunehmen</u>.

(page 59)

1 a Komm herein!

   b Telefonier mal nach Hause!

   c Iss mehr!

   d Sprich Deutsch!

   e Wasch dir die Hände!

   f Schlaf gut!

2 a Schreibt eine Arbeit!

   b Lernt Vokabeln!

   c Arbeitet bitte schneller!

   d Macht rechtzeitig eure Hausaufgaben!

   e Seid ruhig!

   f Passt gut auf!

3 a Besuchen Sie die Museen!

   b Kaufen Sie in den großen Geschäften ein!

   c Benutzen Sie die U-Bahn und Busse!

   d Füttern Sie die Tiere im Zoo!

   e Sehen Sie sich eine Show an!

   f Trinken Sie im Café Kranzler Kaffee!

4 a Seht nicht zu viel fern!

   b Steh früh auf!

   c Seien Sie um 10 Uhr da!

   d Haben Sie keine Angst!

   e Öffne das Fenster!

   f Putzt euch die Nase!

(page 60)

1 a Jürgen <u>steht</u> normalerweise ziemlich früh <u>auf</u>. – present

   b Letzten Dienstag <u>hat</u> er den Bus <u>verpasst</u>. – perfect

   c Er <u>hatte</u> seinen Wecker einfach nicht <u>gehört</u>. – pluperfect

   d Er <u>ist</u> zur Bushaltestelle <u>gerannt</u>. – perfect

   e Vielleicht <u>würde</u> er den Bus noch <u>erreichen</u>. – conditional

   f Der Bus <u>war</u> aber schon <u>abgefahren</u>. – pluperfect

g Er <u>musste</u> auf den nächsten Bus <u>warten</u>. – imperfect + infinitive

h Am Wochenende <u>wird</u> er sich einen besseren Wecker <u>kaufen</u>! – future

2 a Ich stehe samstags spät auf.

b Sie nimmt ein Bad.

c Du telefonierst mit einem Freund.

d Er trifft sich mit ihr.

e Ihr kauft euch ein Eis.

f Du fährst nach Hause.

g Wir sehen ein bisschen fern.

3 a Ich bin nach Griechenland gefahren.

b Wir haben in einem Hotel gewohnt.

c Das Essen war gut.

d Habt ihr viele Ruinen besichtigt?

e Man konnte sich am Strand sonnen.

f Wir mussten leider arbeiten.

g Er ist morgens um 4 Uhr angekommen.

4 a Ich <u>werde</u> viel Geld gewinnen.

b Das <u>würde</u> toll sein!

c Wir <u>werden</u> uns neue Kleidung <u>kaufen</u>.

d Sie <u>würde(n)</u> lange auf Partys <u>bleiben</u>.

e Wann <u>würdet</u> ihr <u>aufstehen</u>?

f Was <u>werden</u> Sie als Beruf <u>machen</u>?

g Ich <u>würde</u> freiwillig <u>arbeiten</u>.

(page 61)

1 a Basel <u>liegt</u> im Norden der Schweiz.

b Drei Städte in der Schweiz, Deutschland und Frankreich <u>teilen</u> sich den Flughafen.

c Viele weltberühmte Pharma-Industrien <u>haben</u> ihren Sitz in der Stadt.

d Die Altstadt <u>hat</u> schöne alte Gebäude.

e Es <u>gibt</u> viele Besucher im Februar wegen Fasnacht.

f Alt und Jung <u>feiern</u> bis spät in die Nacht.

g Man <u>kann</u> jeden Tag große Schiffe und kleine Boote auf dem Rhein sehen.

h Die Häuser, Wohnungen und Geschäfte am Ufer des Rheins <u>haben</u> einen schönen Blick auf den Fluss.

2 a <u>Der Sommer</u> ist meistens ziemlich heiß in Basel.

b Trotz der Industrie finden <u>wir</u> die Stadt einfach super.

c <u>Es</u> gibt vier offizielle Sprachen in der Schweiz.

d In diesem nördlichen Teil der Schweiz spricht <u>man</u> immer Deutsch.

e <u>Der Schweizer Akzent und einige Wörter</u> sind ganz anders als in Deutschland.

f Abends haben <u>die Basler</u> eine große Auswahl an Freizeitaktivitäten.

3 a Jeden Sommer fahren wir in die Schweiz.

b In den schönen Bergen gibt es frische Luft.

c Den ganzen Tag kann man mit Freunden wandern.

d Nur vom Reisebus sehen viele ausländische Touristen die Schweiz.

e Für Wassersport sind die wunderschönen Seen sehr beliebt.

f Nächstes Jahr wollen meine Cousins und ich auf einer Sommerrodelbahn Schlitten fahren.

4 a Mein älterer Bruder <u>wohnt</u> seit acht Jahren in Basel.

b Jedes Wochenende im Winter <u>geht</u> er in die Berge zum Snowboarden.

c Mit der Bahn und dem Bus <u>dauert</u> die Fahrt etwa drei Stunden.

d Leider <u>hatte</u> seine Freundin letzten Februar einen Unfall.

e Sie <u>kann</u> immer noch nicht gut laufen.

f Meine Freundin und ich <u>wollen</u> nächsten Winter mit ihm snowboarden.

(page 62)

1 a Ich arbeite im Sommer mit einer Freundin in einem Freizeitpark.

b Familien fahren im Sommer mit ihren Kindern an den Strand.

c Ich kann jedes Wochenende mit meinen Freunden im Park Rollschuh laufen.

d Mein englischer Brieffreund hat letzten August mit seiner Familie eine Ferienwohnung direkt am Meer gemietet.

e Wir sind jeden Tag mit dem Rad durch die Stadt gefahren.

f Ich muss jeden Abend sehr hart im Café arbeiten.

2 a Mit ihren Kindern fahren Familien im Sommer an den Strand.

b Jedes Wochenende kann ich mit Freunden im Park Rollschuh laufen.

c Eine Ferienwohnung direkt am Meer hat mein Brieffreund gemietet.

d Mit dem Rad sind wir jeden Tag durch die Stadt gefahren.

e Jeden Abend muss ich sehr hart im Café arbeiten.

3 a In Berlin, der größten Stadt Deutschlands, wohnen jetzt ungefähr 3,4 Millionen Menschen.

b Meine Schwester studiert seit zwei Jahren sehr hart in der Hochschule in Dortmund.

c Nach Innsbruck kommen viele Touristen im Juli mit Reisebussen.

d Meine Brieffreundin wohnt seit drei Jahren mit ihren Großeltern in Bayern.

e An der Ostsee kann man jeden Sommer Strandkörbe für die Familie mieten.

f Der Physiker Albert Einstein zog 1932 mit seiner Familie nach Amerika.

(page 63)

1 a Bastian isst immer etwas Gesundes, und er fühlt sich viel besser deswegen.

b Die Stadt Hamburg ist sehr groß, aber sie ist trotzdem sehr freundlich.

c Ich bin ein paar Mal nach Berlin gefahren, denn die Stadt gefällt mir sehr.

d Heute Abend gehen wir ins Kino, oder vielleicht könnten wir zum Bowling gehen.

e Florian lernt jetzt Mathe, aber nächstes Jahr wird er das nicht mehr machen.

2 (suggested answers)

a aber – Young people nowadays want to earn a lot, but they don't want to work hard.

b denn – Malena wants to become a vet, for she likes animals so much.

c aber – At school Karin didn't work much, but as an apprentice she's very hard-working.

d oder/und/aber – Her brother wants to study sport, or/and/but perhaps he's going into the army.

e aber/und – He works in a sport centre, but/and he doesn't get any money for it.

f und – Life in the army can be hard, and sometimes it's very dangerous.

3 a C, **b** S, **c** S, **d** C, **e** S, **f** S, **g** C, **h** S

(page 64)

4 a Ich esse jede Woche Fisch, weil das gut für die Gesundheit ist.

b Wir fahren nicht gern Rad, wenn es stark regnet.

c Ich bleibe noch eine Stunde hier, während du mit Jens nach Hause fährst.

d Sie schreiben alles deutlich auf, damit wir die Arbeit besser verstehen.

5 a Mir ist schlecht, obwohl ich heute nicht zu viel gegessen habe.

b Mein Freund ist nicht zufrieden, dass er keine Süßigkeiten essen darf.

c Alle sind aufgestanden, als er ins Zimmer gekommen ist.

d Ich warte unten im Wohnzimmer, während er sich für die Party umzieht.

e Er weiß nicht, ob wir den Bus verpassen werden.

6 a Während die Heizung in der Schule nicht funktioniert, dürfen die Schüler zu Hause bleiben.

b Obwohl sie heute keine Schule hat, steht sie früh auf.

c Wenn du nicht aufpasst, wirst du zu viele Fehler machen.

d Als die Direktorin plötzlich vor uns stand, hatten alle Angst.

(page 65)

1 (main verbs in bold)

a Sie **hat** mir das Bild zum Geburtstag geschenkt. – neut., acc., sing.

b Der Kuchen **war** für unsere Gäste. – masc., nom., sing.

c Unser Auto **steht** jetzt in der Werkstatt. – fem., dat., sing.

d Unsere Katze **sitzt** auf dem Stuhl. – masc., dat., sing.

e Ich **fahre** mit diesen Freunden nach Wien. – masc., dat., pl.

2 a Ich liebe das Bild, das sie mir zum Geburtstag geschenkt hat.

b Wir haben den Kuchen gegessen, der für unsere Gäste war.

c Die Werkstatt, in der unser Auto jetzt steht, hat eben angerufen.

d Gehört Ihnen der Stuhl, auf dem unsere Katze sitzt?

e Ich gebe eine Party für die Freunde, mit denen ich nach Wien fahre.

3 a Er hat mir Blumen geschickt, was mich sehr gefreut hat.

b Wir haben keinen Saft mehr, was nicht wieder passieren darf.

c Anja hat eine schlechte Note in Mathe, was kaum zu glauben ist.

d Der Hund hat deine Hausaufgaben gefressen, was ich unglaublich finde.

4 a Wir machen eine Stadtrundfahrt, die zwei Stunden dauert.

b Der Bus war sehr unbequem, was mich erstaunt hat.

c Ich habe mich mit einer netten Dame unterhalten, die aus Dresden kommt.

d Ich wusste nicht, wo Dresden war, was mich geärgert hat.

e Die Dame zeigte mir eine Karte, auf der wir Dresden finden konnten.

(page 66)

1 (suggested answers)

a Andrea will sich einen Film ansehen, obwohl sie früh ins Bett gehen muss.

b In der Schule darf man nicht laufen, weil es gefährlich ist.

c Morgen will ich ausgehen, weil das Wetter warm sein wird.

d Malik muss neue Fußballschuhe kaufen, obwohl er es sich nicht leisten kann.

e Herr X möchte Präsident werden, obwohl das nie geschehen wird.

2 **a** gewusst, abgefahren, **b** gespielt, hatten, **c** geregnet, hat, mitgenommen, **d** gesehen, habt, gewonnen, **e** gegangen, war, sind

3 **a** Der Wolf, der die Oma schon gefressen hat, will auch Rotkäppchen fressen.

b Hast du den tollen Computer gesehen, den ich mir kaufen werde?

c Wenn meine Eltern in Berlin angekommen sind, sollen sie mich anrufen.

d Während ihr euch am Strand amüsiert habt, habe ich im Krankenhaus gelegen.

e Was willst du machen, wenn der Regen aufgehört hat?

(page 67)

1 **a** neununddreißig, zweiundfünfzig, dreiundsiebzig, einundneunzig, vierundvierzig

b (ein)hundertfünfundachtzig

c siebentausendzweihundertachtundsechzig

d neun Millionen achthundertsechsund-siebzigtausendfünfhundertdreiundvierzig

2 **a** siebzehn Komma fünf Prozent

b drei Komma vier Millionen Einwohner

c neunundneunzig Komma neun Prozent

d siebenunddreißig Komma fünf Grad Celsius

3 **a** sechzehn Euro vierzig

b siebenundzwanzig Euro achtzig

c ein Euro fünfundneunzig

d (ein)hundertzwölf Franken dreißig

e eintausendfünfhundertsechs Franken fünfzig

(page 68)

1 **a** der siebte Tag, **b** in der elften Klasse, **c** zum zwanzigsten Mal, **d** das achtzehnte Jahrhundert

2 **a** mein 16. Geburtstag, **b** der 44. Präsident, **c** in der 13. Klasse, **d** am 12. Mai

3 **a** ein Drittel, **b** ein Fünftel, **c** ein Achtel, **d** ein Zwanzigstel

4 **1** f, **2** d, **3** j, **4** e, **5** i, **6** a, **7** h, **8** b, **9** g, **10** c

(page 69)

1 **a** Der erste August ist der Schweizer Nationalfeiertag.

b Der dritte Oktober ist der Tag der Deutschen Einheit.

c Der sechsundzwanzigste Oktober ist der österreichische Nationalfeiertag.

d Der siebenundzwanzigste Januar ist Mozarts Geburtstag.

2 **a** Am vierzehnten Februar.

b Am neunten November neunzehnhundertneunundachtzig.

c Am sechsundzwanzigsten März 1827.

d Vom vierundzwanzigsten bis zum sechsundzwanzigsten Dezember.

e Am einunddreißigsten Dezember.

f (open-ended)

g (open-ended)

3 **a** Hamburg, den zehnten Mai

b Ulm, den fünfzehnten Juni

c Köln, den einundzwanzigsten Juli

d Wien, den siebten April

e Bern, den dreißigsten September

f München, den achtundzwanzigsten Februar

4 open-ended

(page 70)

1 **a** drei Uhr fünfzehn − Viertel nach drei

b fünf Uhr zwanzig − zwanzig nach fünf

c sechs Uhr dreißig − halb sieben

d zwanzig Uhr fünfundvierzig − Viertel vor neun

e neun Uhr fünfzig − zehn vor zehn

f dreiundzwanzig Uhr zehn − zehn nach elf

2 open-ended